Cichlids

Cichlids

Understanding Angelfish, Oscars, Discus, and Others

David Alderton

Irvine, California

Published in 2003 by BowTie Press
3 Burroughs, Irvine, CA 92618
www.bowtiepress.com
Fish Keeping Made Easy is an imprint of BowTie Press

Produced by Andromeda Oxford Limited
11–13 The Vineyard, Abingdon
Oxon OX14 3PX.
www.andromeda.co.uk

Project Director: Graham Bateman
Managing Editor: Shaun Barrington
Design: D and N DTP and Editorial Services
Editorial Assistant: Rita Demetriou
Picture Manager: Claire Turner
Production: Clive Sparling
Indexer: Janet Dudley

Picture on page 2: *Hemichromis fasciatus.*

Library of Congress Cataloging-in-Publication Data
Alderton, David, 1956-
    Cichlids : understanding your angelfish, oscars, discus, and others/by
      David Alderton.
      p. cm.
    Includes bibliographical references (p.   ).
    ISBN 1-931993-10-6 (hardback : alk. paper)
    1. Cichlids. I. Title.
SF458.C5 A58 2002
639.3'774--dc21   2002008845

Photographic Credits
Ardea 100–101; Liz Bomford/Ardea 16–17; Peter Steyn/Ardea 27; Jane Burton/Bruce Coleman Collection 90, 95;
Michael Freeman/Bruce Coleman Collection 7; © www.Hippocampus-Bildarchiv.de 2, 13, 15–16b, 22–24, 35t, 39, 42,
58, 62–64, 68–70, 73, 77b, 81, 93, 97, 102–103, 107, 112, 120, 127b, 128b, 130, 131b, 132t, 133t, 135t; Anthony
Bannister/Natural History Photographic Agency 71, 111; T. Kitchen and V. Hurst/Natural History Photographic Agency
94; Georgette Douwma/Nature Picture Library 110; Max Gibbs/Photomax 3, 6, 9, 10t, 12, 14, 19–21, 25–26, 28–34,
35b–38, 40–41, 44–56, 60, 65–66, 75–77t, 78–80, 86–88, 91, 98, 105, 113–119, 121–127t, 128t, 129, 131t, 132b,
133b–134, 135b–137; M.P. and C. Piednoir 82; F. Schafer 10b; Jane Burton/Warren Photographic 57, 67, 74; Kim
Taylor/Warren Photographic 83–84. All artwork by Mick Loates.

Color origination by A.T. Color, Milan
Printed and bound in China

14 13 12 11 10   3 4 5 6 7 8 9 10

Contents

Nature and Nurture

It is no surprise that cichlids have become one of the most popular groups of aquarium fish. Apart from their sheer variety of color and shape, their breeding habits are really quite amazing. Within the home aquarium, you can observe many fascinating aspects of cichlid biology at close quarters, particularly the parental care displayed by these fish toward their eggs and offspring.

The diversity that exists within the cichlid family means that a clear understanding of their natural environments and behavior is essential in order to keep them successfully. Their geographical origins will give you a fairly accurate insight into their requirements. And an understanding of their natural habitats is essential for breeding success. For these reasons, this book deliberately returns wherever possible to the original home of the species described.

Central American cichlids typically need relatively hard, alkaline water conditions. In contrast, those originating from further south in the Amazonian region live in waters with a quite different chemical makeup, which is soft and acidic. There are some cichlids from the northwest of South America, however, such as the green terror (*Aequidens rivulatus*), inhabiting waters that more closely approximate to those of their Central American relatives.

⏷ Male South African or dwarf copper mouthbrooders (*Pseudocrenilabrus philander dispersus*) will burrow more frequently in the substrate as the time for spawning nears, creating pits.

Many American cichlids grow to a large size, and their territorial aggression means that in the confines of an aquarium, they need to be kept on their own. Only the small dwarf cichlids, forming the *Apistogramma* genus, can be housed safely in a community aquarium of other non-aggressive fish from the Amazonian region. Even then, males should be kept apart from each other.

In Africa too, cichlids can be found in very different water conditions from one area to another. The Rift lakes of East Africa for example, home to many of these fish, are not all the same. Both Lake Victoria and Lake Malawi have water that is moderately hard, typically 8-10dH, but whereas Lake Victoria has a pH reading of 7-7.5, the Malawi waters measure pH 7.5-8. The waters of Lake Tanganyika are both slightly harder, with a dH of 15-20, and also more alkaline, with a pH of 8-8.5. The breeding habits of the cichlids from this lake are also more diverse, with some spawning in the substrate rather than being mouthbrooders.

The actual habitats within these lakes are similar however, forming several recognizable ecosystems. The shoreline area may be strewn with rockwork, creating the environment favored by the popular mbuna group of cichlids inhabiting Lake Malawi. In other parts of the lakes, the shoreline is sandy, with weedbeds, while out above the essentially lifeless depths of these lakes is open water. This area is home to a number of fast-swimming, predatory members of the group.

There are cichlids from the rainforests of West Africa as well that need water conditions corresponding to those found in the Amazonian area. As befits a group whose ancestors originated from the marine environment, so certain cichlids even require brackish water conditions. This applies notably to the Asian chromides (*Etroplus* species). The information within the following pages will give a clear insight into the individual needs of the most popular groups of these marvelous fish, helping you to make your choice successfully, knowing from the outset what is required. And the discussion of natural environment and behavior is not purely for practical purposes: It surely adds to the satisfaction and enjoyment of cichlid keeping to acknowledge and understand their wild nature and thus be able to interpret their behavior in the aquarium.

The waters of the Amazon provide a soft, acidic habitat for a variety of cichlids.

CHAPTER 1

Where in the World?

The cichlids—pronounced "sick-lids"—represent one of the largest and most diverse groups of fish today. Their variance in color and appearance has boosted their popularity as aquarium fish. There are at least 1,500 species of cichlid, although no one is exactly sure of the total figure: many as yet undocumented species may await discovery, particularly in the lakes of Africa's Great Rift Valley.

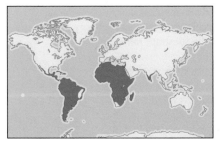

⬆ Cichlids are found predominantly in the southern hemisphere, notably in Africa and the Americas.

Most cichlids inhabit freshwater, but some species can range into brackish or even salt water. Representatives of the group are present on all continents, with the exception of Europe and Australia. They are found predominantly south of the Tropic of Cancer, with the Texas cichlid (*Herichthys cyanoguttatus*) from North America being the most northerly representative of the family.

Cichlids, as a group, are known for their varied body shape and size. Some cichlids, such as the popular discus (*Symphysodon aequifasciatus*), have a flattened body shape, whereas other species are tubular. It is therefore not easy to recognize a cichlid by its appearance. Nevertheless, a few of the group's distinguishing features can be identified by a careful external examination.

TYPICAL FEATURES

Perhaps one of the most obvious features is the presence of a single rather than a double pair of nostrils above the top lip. The anal fin on the underside of the body has at least three bony spines, while the dorsal fin running down the back has a combination of spines at the front and softer wavy rays behind. Males can use this fin for display purposes, thanks to its flexibility and the fact that it is often embellished at its rear.

If you look closely at the side of a cichlid's body, you will also notice that the lateral line, visible as a lighter streak extending down the body, is not continuous (as in most fish) but is split into two distinct parts. The anterior section, beginning near the top of the gill cover or operculum, runs down to a point above the anal fin. The lower, disjunctive rear portion of this jelly-filled sensory canal then continues back as far as the caudal peduncle, at the base of the tail fin. There are exceptions, notably in the case of the narrow-bodied cichlids such as *Teleogramma* species. Their streamlined shape is an adaptation to life in fast-flowing sections of the River Zaire.

Some hidden characteristics set cichlids apart from other fish. These include how the intestinal tract connects to the right-hand side of the fish's stomach. In other groups, where a recognizable stomach is present, the exit point is to be found on the left of this organ.

The ear structure of cichlids is also a distinguishing feature. Although there is obviously no external ear canal, the ears of all bony fish (including cichlids) are present where they would be expected, behind the eyes. They are not used primarily for hearing sounds, however: the lateral line picks up sound waves and vibrations in the water. Instead, the three semicircular canals forming each ear are used as organs of balance. At the base of each semicircular canal are hard structures called otoliths, which move in response to the fish's positioning, giving a clear indication of its orientation. The largest of these otoliths is called the saggita, and it has a very distinctive furrow and shape.

LINKS WITH THE SEA

Cichlids form part of a grouping known as labroids, with their closest relatives being marine fish. They include damselfishes (Pomacentridae), wrasses (Labridae), and parrotfish (Scaridae), all of which are well known to marine aquarists. What is particularly interesting is the way in which many of the cichlid species found in the Rift Valley lakes of Africa resemble marine fish in appearance. This is not to suggest that they originated from a marine ancestor, as was initially believed following their discovery in Lake Tanganyika. Instead it suggests convergent evolution. Many cichlid species in the Rift Valley lakes have been subjected to similar selection pressures as those imposed on reef fish. As a result, they have developed corresponding forms. It is not just the mouthparts that have developed accordingly, but the whole shape of their bodies. There are cichlids with matching outlines corresponding to groupers, tuna, and even gobies.

◑ The single pair of nostrils, which is a characteristic of members of this group of fish, is clearly visible in this head-on portrait of a turquoise discus (*Symphysodon aequifasciatus*).

9

⊕ Cichlids are closely related to marine fish like this shimmering parrot wrasse (*Cirrhilabrus rubrimarginatus*).

A number of these fish have become brightly colored, just like many reef fish, which is why they are sometimes described as freshwater coral fish. However, those cichlid species that are free-swimming (rather than occupying a localized lake habitat) have shed their bright coloration. Their silvery sheen helps to conceal their presence from above. Visibility can be remarkable in these waters, with the clarity being as much as 72ft (22m) in the still waters of Lake Tanganyika.

⊕ Lake Tanganyika in the East African Rift Valley has become home to a remarkable diversity of cichlids. This is a view of Kasaba bay, Zambia.

Based on their distribution today, it appears that the original ancestors of today's cichlids probably started to evolve as a group around 160 million years ago, on the huge southern mass known as Gondwanaland, but much of their early development has to be speculative, in the absence of fossilized remains. The first clear evidence of a recognizable cichlid species is much later, dating to the Oligocene epoch, about 26 million years ago.

By the Oligocene, South America was already drifting apart from Africa, which is believed to be the homeland of these fish. The last link

Ancestral Rockies

PANTHALASSA OCEAN

between these landmasses was a connection extending between West Africa and Brazil, close to the Equator, at a time when the water levels in the world's oceans were much lower than they are today. This connection would have allowed fish to swim between these areas, allowing colonization of the southern continent to take place.

⬇ The division of the old supercontinent of Gondwana, or Gondwanaland, at the end of the Jurassic period helps to explain the distribution of cichlids around the globe today. Those massive rifts are beginning to create South America, Africa and the Middle East. Once the landmasses have separated, American and African cichlids develop separately: but almost certainly, they are all descendants of Gondwana fish.

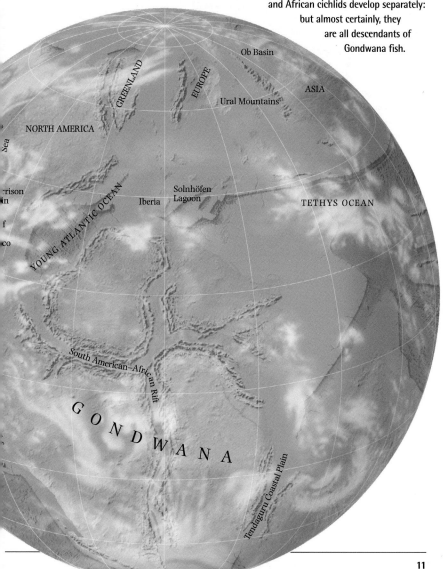

They may have crossed via river estuaries, perhaps entering salt water for short periods of time. The early cichlids may have been even better suited to survival in salt water at that stage, as they were descended from marine ancestors, and then started to spread up the rivers of what is now South America. The other possibility is that marine ancestors of the group entered both Africa and the Americas, and evolved independently, but this is thought to be less likely, given the distribution pattern of the family today, especially in Asia.

The Amazonian area in the Oligocene was a massive lake, and then as this huge river formed, resulting in a fall in water level, so populations of cichlids probably became more isolated in its tributaries. They then gradually evolved into distinctive species, with their own individual characteristics.

Some of these early cichlids moved north, into Central America. At this stage, a narrow isthmus connected the central and southern continents. It broke up about 30 million years ago, with its remnants being represented today by the islands of Cuba and Hispaniola. Cichlids that had been present in the former Central American isthmus then found themselves in what is now the Caribbean; the fossilized remains of a species called *Cichlasoma woodringi* have been found on the island of Haiti.

This breakup left South America marooned as a separate island until a connection was reestablished by further geological upheaval approximately three million years ago. Those cichlids now native to Central America arrived at about that time. They probably spread quickly, as they are known to radiate out into favorable habitats.

ADAPTING TO THE ENVIRONMENT

Nowhere is this ability to adapt more evident than in East Africa. One of the most remarkable aspects of cichlid biology is the way in which these fish respond quickly to environmental pressures, as is apparent from the populations occurring in the lakes of East Africa. Competition for food has been a very significant and rapid determining factor in the evolution of cichlid species worldwide, particularly in lake habitats. The fish will reproduce rapidly, and in the relative absence of predators, so their reproductive potential means that their numbers will soon be limited by the available supply of food. This pressure for food led cichlids to become increasingly specialized in their feeding habits, diversifying in this way to ensure their survival.

⬇ Fishing in the Congo. While cichlids are popular aquarium occupants, many species are also important as food fish, with some larger species such as *Tilapia* even being bred commercially for this purpose today.

Other factors come into play, notably the reproductive behavior of the fish. This starts with mate selection and continues through egg laying and hatching. One of the fascinating characteristics of cichlids is that, as far as is known, all display a degree of parental care that is unparalleled across any other group of fish. Breeding becomes a more reliable event as a consequence.

Water differences

Within Africa itself, the populations of cichlids differ from one another in their biology and their native environments. Those found on the west of the continent are, not surprisingly, closely allied to those occurring in the Americas in terms of their environmental needs. They inhabit rivers where the water chemistry is soft and acidic, whereas cichlids on the eastern side of the continent, which are believed to be descended from them, are found in hard, alkaline waters.

Relatively few cichlids occur in Asia, which is a reflection of the timing and the way in which the continental landmasses split up at what was a relatively early stage in the cichlids' evolutionary process. The areas of the Middle East, Madagascar, and India were closely positioned along what is now the east coast of Africa, in the old supercontinent of Gondwanaland. Small populations of cichlids "migrated" as India and the Middle East drifted north to link with mainland Asia. Madagascar, on the other hand, stayed close to Africa, but as a distinct island. This explains why the cichlids of Madagascar are more closely allied to Indian species, rather than to those occurring on mainland Africa. Scientists also believe these species to be representative of the most primitive cichlid lineages.

➊ Orange (*right*) and red chromide (*Etroplus maculatus* and var.)

THE CRATER OF EVOLUTION

Study of the cichlids occurring in the lakes of East Africa has excited evolutionary biologists for nearly 150 years. The explorers David Livingstone and John Kirk obtained cichlid specimens from Lake Nyasa (now known as Lake Malawi), while on a quest to discover the source of the River Nile in 1861.

Even today, no one knows exactly how many different species of cichlid are present within this particular lake. Estimates suggest that there could be anywhere from 1,000 to1,600 species, although barely 500 have yet been described by zoologists. The huge range of speciation—the process by which species develop—that has occurred within this single lake is remarkable. To give this some perspective, there is actually a bigger range of cichlids within this single lake than all the freshwater fish species found in North and Central America combined.

The Rift Valley extends for nearly 3,000 miles (5,000km), from the Jordan Valley down through Africa as far south as Mozambique. A geological fault has caused the land to sink, a process that continues today. This sinking has created a remarkably consistent trench, with the associated valleys in East Africa typically measuring 25–34 miles (40–55km) wide.

Another distinctive feature of the Rift Valley is the presence of about 20 lakes, rather than rivers, running down its length. Some of these lakes resemble inland seas in their depth and extent. The three major lakes in East Africa of particular significance with regard to their cichlid populations are Lake Victoria, which is the most northerly of the group, with Lake Tanganyika next, followed by Lake Malawi (formerly Lake Nyasa), which lies farther south.

Lake Tanganyika is at least 6 million years old. It has become deeper since the Pleistocene, some 750,000 years ago, when a major volcanic eruption caused water from Lake Kivu to flow in from the north. Today, Lake Tanganyika descends to a maximum depth of about 4,900ft (1,500m). Lake Malawi dates back approximately 2 million years, and has gradually expanded southward. It is roughly 1,950ft (600m) at its deepest point.

The youngest and shallowest of the lakes is Victoria, which was formed as a result of the land upheavals in the region during the Pleistocene. This altered river flows in the west of the region, causing them to pool together, creating this massive body of water. It is

❶ Cichlids have developed similarities in appearance, even though they have evolved in different localities, as shown here by Fuelleborn's cichlid (*Labeotropheus fulleborni*) from Lake Malawi (*left*), Burton's mouthbrooder (*Astatotilapia burtoni* "blue") from Lake Tanganyika (*below left*) and a new Haplochromis form from Lake Victoria that has yet to be scientifically classified (*below*). Sorting out the different relationships within this group of fish is an ongoing task for zoologists.

➲ The ornate julie (*Julidochromis ornatus*) is often referred to as one of the "dwarf" julies.

➊ Striped julies (*Julidochromis regani*) occur around the rocky shoreline of Lake Tanganyika. They require an aquarium matching their natural environment, with rocks and open sandy areas.

➲ Cichlid taxonomy is often contentious. These fish may be considered a subspecies of the Egyptian mouth-brooder (*Pseudo-crenilabrus multicolor*); others argue they are a distinct species.

now up to 330ft (100m) deep in places. The sheer scale of these lakes is such that they are hard to visualize. Lake Victoria, for example, occupies an area the size of the state of Maine.

Being the oldest of the lakes, and colonized more effectively at the outset, Lake Tanganyika displays the greatest diversity of endemic cichlid species. The range in size of the cichlids occurring here is also unparalleled. The smallest is about 1.75in (3.75cm) long. *Boulengerochromis microlepis*, on the other hand, is the largest cichlid species in the world, measuring approximately 36in (91cm) long.

It is no coincidence that Lake Victoria may contain more cichlid species than other lakes. Firstly, it offers greater areas of habitat. Both Lake Tanganyika and Lake Malawi are set in deep troughs, and although they cover a large area, their oxygen-deprived depths offer no suitable habitat for cichlids. There is no effective wind movement in these sheltered areas to stir the water, increasing its oxygen level. The positioning of Lake Victoria in more open country, coupled with its shallower structure, means that waves roll across its surface, increasing the oxygen uptake into the water.

VARYING WATER LEVELS

One of the significant differences between the African Rift lakes and seas, is the fact that the water level in the lakes depends to a great extent on rainfall. It has varied significantly as a consequence, even in the recent past. Today, for example, Lake Malawi is as much as 500ft (150m) higher than it was during the mid-nineteenth century. When Lake Victoria started to form, it flooded the area partially, creating what would have been a series of smaller lakes. These probably reached a maximum depth approximately 100ft (30m) above the level of today, but then about 12,500–15,000 years ago, the water level fell dramatically. Carbon dating of lake deposits suggests that it may have even dried up completely at this stage.

🔼 Water levels within the Rift Valley lakes still vary from year to year, as seen here by this flooding on the shoreline of Lake Malawi, but the shifts are not as dramatic today as they have been in the past.

Such an event would have wiped out all the fish living there. If this theory is correct, then it means that today's many cichlid species must have evolved in what in evolutionary terms is equivalent to a fraction of a millisecond, once the lake reformed. This evolutionary mystery helps to explain why Rift Valley cichlids have become so fascinating for evolutionary biologists and fish keepers alike.

Analysis of the mitochondrial DNA of 14 species of cichlid drawn from nine recognized genera (a reliable indicator of population divergences) reveals that these fish showed far less genetic variation than exists within the human species. This result reinforces the likelihood that all these cichlid species are recently derived from a single ancestral form. It is also a direct reflection of where these lakes formed—near the headwaters of rivers, where there were relatively few fish species present to populate them in the first instance.

It is harder to fathom how these ancestral cichlids, entering the lakes from the surrounding rivers, subsequently developed in the early stages. It is likely the early cichlids were fairly nonspecific in their habits, and probably fed on a vegetarian diet. But other colonizations of smaller lakes give tantalizing clues as to how this evolutionary process probably began.

Evolutionary examples

Lake Barombi lies in a volcanic crater, close to the town of Kumba in the Cameroon. The northern end of the lake is fed by a small stream. This water supply improves the oxygenation of the water in this area, making it a better feeding site. Nutrients will be concentrated close to the surface here, with the current keeping them in suspension. At the opposite end of the lake, however, there is a tendency for sedimentation to occur where water drains from the lake.

Separating these two zones are the steep, craggy sides of the submerged crater, which offer little in the way of feeding possibilities for fish. The ancestral fish population seems to have diverged initially at each end of the lake, with the northern cichlids being surface-feeders, in contrast to the southern bottom-feeders. Each range gradually expanded, ultimately overlapping with each other.

Where *Konia* cichlids encountered *Stomatepia* colonizing their southern stronghold, they reacted by moving into the shallows in this part of the lake. When they crossed into the northern area, the *Konia* fish settled in deeper water, to avoid competition with their northerly cousins. This process would then, in effect, create four species. Lake Barombi now supports both the original *Konia* population (*Konia eisentrauti*) and its deep-water counterpart (*Konia dikume*). The latter species has tremendous hemoglobin reserves, enabling it to dive into what is virtually deoxygenated water in the depths of the lake, to feed on fly larvae.

A further split has occurred in the case of the inshore *Stomatepia* population, based on the cichlids' diurnal activity pattern. There is now a species that is active during hours of daylight, and another that prefers to hunt at night, in addition to their deep-water counterpart, *Stomatepia mongo*. Thus five distinctive species of cichlid have evolved from a single ancestor in this small African lake.

Their distributions were affected initially by the environmental conditions and then the development of related forms. This in turn has exerted a selection pressure to avoid competition, what is often described by biologists as adaptive radiation. Species diversify to create and survive in new ecological niches where they face less competition.

Evidence from Lake Tanganyika

Further evidence can be found in the relative shallows of Lake Tanganyika, whose southern shoreline is home to a cichlid known as *Tropheus moorii*, a popular fish with aquarists. It occurs around

◐ Populations of *Tropheus moorii* vary significantly in their appearance, each population having evolved in isolation from neighboring ones.

There are more than 10 currently recognized morphs of *Tropheus moorii*. This is why it is not always enough simply to ask for a particular cichlid from a supplier, especially in the case of those originating from the Rift Valley lakes. You need to confirm the exact type that you are seeking. The names of these fish are often appended with the area of the lake where they or their ancestors originated, which helps to simplify the identification process.

⬆ Red band cichlid (*Tropheus moorii*).

the lake in a number of different localities, with the individual populations being largely separated by physical obstructions such as rockfalls.

Many of these populations are sufficiently isolated to be showing signs of developing on separate lines. Those from the southwest of the lake are quite dark in overall coloration, whereas those obtained in the vicinity of Kiriza, especially males, display a bright yellow band around their bodies. This phenomenon is known as polymorphism, and reflects the way in which the species has diversified through its range, in relative isolation. As to when a morph becomes a distinct species can, however, be a controversial decision.

There would have been a unique series of pressures imposed on these fish, to create the diversity in form and lifestyle that occurs within the cichlid population of the lake today. One key aspect of the cichlid's morphology has contributed to this diversity. Specifically the jaw structure has become more flexible. This is believed to have enabled them to adapt readily to different food and feeding habits, with increasing specialization allowing them to exploit individual niches, free from competition.

Adaptability in the tank

The remarkable way in which cichlids adapt in the face of selection pressures is even now apparent in commercial captive-breeding establishments. It has been noted how the jaw angle has been modified by surface-feeding in some cases, notably of cichlids that are bottom-feeders in the wild state. This change confirms the

LEARNING SKILLS

Another less immediately obvious feature of cichlids—which has been proved in laboratory surroundings and frequently observed in the home aquarium—is their ability to learn, and thus modify their feeding habits easily. It is no coincidence that many cichlids can be taught to feed from the hand. Such opportunism in turn brings survival benefits in the wild, as dramatically revealed by the case of the play dead cichlid (*Nimbochromis livingstonii*). Instead of expending energy on hunting, it simply lies on the sand in Lake Malawi, appearing to be dead and decomposing which attracts other fish as scavengers. They then become its unsuspecting prey, caught unawares by the combination of its appearance and behavior.

↑ Play dead cichlid (*Nimbochromis livingstonii*), also sometimes called the sleeper.

immense plasticity of various members of the family, enabling them to alter their physical appearance within a few generations to take advantage of more favorable environmental conditions. It also carries a warning, as far as breeders of such fish are concerned, because there is almost certainly a trend toward seeking out and breeding the most colorful individuals, irrespective of other traits.

Pollution and vision

Unfortunately the waters of Lake Victoria have become more polluted recently, reducing visibility accordingly. Color distinctions between male fish are no longer as conspicuous to the drab-colored females.

DEPTH AND COLORATION

Coloration has also played a crucial role in the speciation process of Rift Valley cichlids, thanks to their well-developed sense of color vision. In such closely related species, interbreeding is prevented by differences in the coloration of male fish; females can identify partners of their own particular species without difficulty by sight. The visibility of colors to their eyes differs according to depth, being influenced by the available light, with yellow and red shades being more conspicuous at greater depth than blue. It is therefore not surprising that blue males are representative of species occurring in shallower waters.

⬆ The coloration of cichlids can give an idea of the depth at which they are found in the wild. Blue indicates shallower waters.

Hybridization has started to become widespread, with females spawning with males of species that in clearer water they would avoid, in preference for a partner of their own species. The hybrid offspring are themselves fertile, which leads to a more widespread breakdown in the barriers between species as they themselves mature (though, confusingly, you could argue that if the hybrids are fertile, then the parents weren't strictly of different species!). Cichlids from this lake are only kept in aquariums relatively rarely.

⬆ Yellow peacock (*Aulonocara baenschi*) from Lake Malawi. These fish occur in relatively deep water off-shore, seeking shelter among the rocks that litter the sandy bottom in this area of the lake.

Habitat pressures

The impact of the habitat itself is the key to the development of diversity in cichlid populations. Although from above, the Rift Valley lakes may simply appear as vast expanses of water, below the surface, there are many different microhabitats. Some areas are characterized by having a sandy base, whereas other parts are rocky, while weed is prevalent at certain localities, but absent elsewhere. This changing underwater scenery means that fish evolve in these different microhabitats, and are not evenly distributed around

⬆ The Malawi
sandnest builder
(*Protomelas
fenestratus*) needs to
be housed in an
aquarium with a
sandy substrate in
parts, matching its
natural habitat.

the lake. Species with distinctive characteristics are most likely to develop in such areas of relative isolation.

The lack of oxygen in the water restricts colonization of this type of habitat. In the case of Lake Malawi, there is not enough dissolved oxygen down below 820ft (250m) to support life, so the fish here are confined to the upper layers. The breeding behavior of cichlids is geared to this environment, with even the upper reaches in the lake being less well oxygenated than flowing rivers. Some lay their eggs in special pits in sand, guarding them until they hatch. This behavior entails swimming close by to create localized water movement, increasing oxygenation over their nest. Many cichlids from this part of the world engage in mouthbrooding, which keeps their eggs and young fry safe. This reproductive method also has another, less obvious advantage: it oxygenates the eggs as the fish draws in water through its mouth that then flows out over its gills.

The lack of current combined with mouth-brooding behavior has a further long-term effect. The fish are not predisposed to disperse into new areas. Instead, such populations become more isolated, increasing the potential for inbreeding.

Little could Livingstone and Kirk have guessed at the remarkable breeding behaviors of the fish that they brought back to England.

Coloration may have contributed to the diversity of species now to be found in the lake, with females preferring males with the brightest colors in some cases. Other breeding strategies involve complex display patterns. Certain males build elaborate sandcastles, consisting of grains of sand piled up to 4ft (1m) high, in order to attract mates. This has the effect of causing populations to become even more isolated, favoring the development of more species, in accordance with Charles Darwin's theory of sexual selection as a driver of the evolutionary process.

SURVIVAL TODAY

Cichlids in the Rift Valley lakes now face an increasing number of hazards, which are having adverse effects on the survival of these unique piscine communities. Monitoring suggests that most of these problems are linked to human activity. It is quite possible that some unique species, whose appearance and behavior has never been documented, may already have disappeared from the lakes.

What is known is that deforestation, leading to increasing turbidity in the waters of Lake Victoria thanks to the runoff of water, is endangering some cichlids by making the waters more cloudy. This hinders mate recognition, as well as physically changing the underwater environment, with less light leading on to harmful effects on the vegetation here. Chemical pollution may represent a growing threat as well, especially with hopes that oil may lie in this region.

The sensitivity of these unique lake habitats has been further highlighted by the damage arising from the introduction of a related species known as the Nile perch (*Lates niloticus*) into Lake Victoria. This giant fish, growing to the height of a man and weighing as much as 135lb (61kg), has proved to be a vicious predator, capable of wiping out entire native species. These perch were deliberately introduced into the lake, probably during the 1950s. It took several decades for their impact on the cichlid population to become apparent, but by the 1980s, commercial fisheries were recording plummeting cichlid numbers, while catches of Nile perch rose dramatically.

Certain types of cichlid have become particularly vulnerable as a result of the introduction of this species. Nile perch prefer to hunt in open stretches of water, where there is little cover available,

● The Nile perch (*Lates niloticus*) was probably introduced to Lake Victoria for sport fishing, but with devastating consequences for the native cichlids. At the same time, it has produced a massive commercial fishing industry.

so they can home in on their prey more easily. The large predatory cichlids, which were previously the dominant piscine species in such areas of the lake, have suffered severely. But remarkably now, even within this short space of time, there are signs that the surviving populations are adapting to this threat.

Adaptive response

There is evidence that these particular cichlids are becoming smaller in size, allowing them to mature earlier and also, that their reproductive rate is increasing. Females now produce more eggs when they spawn. Such reactions to heavy predation are not unique to cichlids, or indeed fish. Blue whales also responded in this way when human hunting was driving these giant cetaceans to the verge of extinction. It does, however, reflect almost a last attempt by a species to stave off possible extinction.

In Lake Tanganyika, there are predatory species of Nile perch living alongside the very diverse cichlid population, so there is hope that over time, more benign coexistence will occur in Lake Victoria. But the cost, in terms of the loss of undocumented species of cichlid, will never be known.

The delicate environmental balance in these lakes is further emphasized by the effects of the introduction of the aquatic plant known as water hyacinth (*Eichornia crassipes*), which is now most common in Lake Victoria. It spreads very rapidly in calm areas of water, covering the surface. Ironically, it has offered some protection to cichlids against Nile perch, which may not be able to meet their oxygen requirements under this blanket of vegetation.

Humans have also been affected by declining cichlid numbers.

🔽 Water hyacinth (*Eichornia crassipes*) is an introduced species to some African lakes, which can grow rapidly and become a pest.

Excessive commercial fishing in Lake Malawi has had a deleterious effect on the numbers of snail-eating cichlids. As a result, the mollusk population has increased, along with that of the *Schistosoma* parasite. These flukes undergo part of their lifecycle in aquatic snails, and then attack people swimming in the water. They cause the human infection known as schistosomiasis, which is fatal without treatment.

⊕ Fishing with a scoop net on Lake Malawi. This method catches fish in the shallower areas of water.

The incidence of this disease has more than doubled in children around the shores of the lake in 15 years, with this increase being directly attributable to the declining population of cichlids, allowing the snail population to multiply largely unchecked. The situation could become even worse if water hyacinth is allowed to spread unchecked in this lake, as aquatic snails thrive in it, often out of the reach of most fish in the dense mats that this plant forms.

Market newcomers

It was not until the 1950s that the first examples of Rift Valley cichlids were seen in Europe, with interest in these fish growing rapidly in the 1970s. The limited trade that does occur actually has conservation benefits; fish that are exported fetch much higher values than those being caught simply for food. The trade itself provides a valuable income for local people in the area—not just the fishermen, but those involved in acclimatizing and caring for the fish, as well as shipping and transporting them.

Collection sites are now restricted, and given the commercial value attaching to these cichlids, there is increased interest in monitoring their populations and conserving their habitat. Not all cichlids are caught in this way—the majority of those sold in aquatic stores are now being commercially bred.

CHAPTER 2

The Different Groups

*The most obvious source for particular cichlids will be your local aquatic store. Many stock a reasonable selection, usually of the most common species such as angelfish (**Pterophyllum** spp.) and discus (**Symphysodon** spp.), along with various Rift Valley cichlids. Fish keeping magazines can help you to track down more specialist stores for an ever wider choice of cichlids.*

You can use the same magazines—or fish keeping web sites—to locate a specialist breeder. This route can be especially useful if you are seeking one of the more unusual species or color varieties. You may have to be patient, however, because there is no guarantee that the breeder will have stock for sale. Also, you need to start out with unrelated individuals for breeding purposes.

🔽 This is a female member of the *Protomelas* genus; but unless you read the label in the shop, how would you know? And would you know what kind of aquarium conditions it requires? Do not be too proud to seek expert advice.

Whether or not you intend to buy immediately, you should consider joining a specialist society. That way you can be kept up to date with what is happening in the cichlid world, through contacts with fellow enthusiasts around the globe. With Internet access you can even monitor natural cichlid habitats by means of webcam broadcasts.

MAKING CHOICES

Choosing healthy fish in the first instance is vital. You may need to be prepared to pay slightly more for a compatible breeding pair, for example. Although this can be a wise investment, it is just

about impossible to be certain of the age of adult cichlids unless the vendor has kept them before they reached maturity. There is a slight risk with an adult pair that the male may settle more quickly in new surroundings than his partner, and may harry her initially if she is not ready to start spawning.

In many cases, there may only be young cichlids available. Bear in mind that their appearance can sometimes differ quite radically from that of adults. In the case of *Tropheus duboisi* as an example, the adults are blackish overall, with a colored band behind their pectoral fins. Juveniles in contrast are also black, but with prominent white spots over their entire bodies.

You may sometimes be offered wild-caught cichlids, but most are likely to be bred on fish farms or by enthusiasts. For Rift Valley cichlids, consider buying a group of the same fish, because there is no guarantee that they will be available again from the same locality in the future. A number of the distinctive forms are named after the area of the lake where they originated, and a knowledgeable dealer will be able to advise you about the available stock.

It may also be possible to place an order for a particular species that is not in stock, but might be available from a supplier. You need to be sure of the terms you are entering into with such a commitment: A dealer's current stock may be excellent, but there is no absolute guarantee that any fish that you order will be as healthy.

Recognizing healthy cichlids will take careful observation, so always give yourself adequate time to check the fish. It may be easier to do this in a store at a relatively quiet time of day, rather than a busy weekend afternoon. It is not just a matter of how the fish look, but also how they behave. This is especially significant if you are hoping to spot a likely pair among a group of young cichlids. Many stores offer cichlids at this age because they will require less space than adult pairs, and also simply because they are more readily obtainable.

The natural coloration of fish such as these green discus (*Symphysodon aequifasciatus*) is often more subdued than in the case of domesticated strains. This is a pair, though sexing discus is notoriously difficult.

First things first

In the first instance, take a look at all the fish in the tank. This is important because if one or two are showing obvious signs of white spot (see page 121), for example, then all the fish will probably be

infected. If you buy any, you will introduce this parasite to your aquarium, representing a hazard also to healthy fish already there.

By looking at the individuals, you may be able to spot differences that may allow you to pick out a pair with some certainty. Once a fish has caught your eye, look at it more closely. It should be active and able to swim without any apparent difficulty, displaying no signs of damage to its fins. Healthy fish are well colored and relatively plump, showing no sign of emaciation that is usually indicative of a chronic illness. Check the eyes are not cloudy or inflamed, and that there are no missing scales or other damage to the sides of the body. Be sure to see the fish from both sides, as otherwise you could easily overlook a problem of this type. Ask about the origins of the fish, and especially whether they have been dewormed: Wild-caught cichlids are more susceptible to such parasites.

As a final check, look more closely at the fish you have chosen when they are netted for you, bearing in mind that you may need several females and only one male—in the case of the *Apistogramma* dwarf cichlids, for example—rather than individual pairs. Each cichlid should be accommodated in a separate plastic bag for the trip home, because they may disagree violently under these circumstances. This applies especially in the case of those that are territorial or polygamous by nature. If a male is confined with a single female, she could be injured or even killed in the bag.

Basic preparations

Always head home directly with your fish, so they can be transferred back to an aquarium without delay. If the weather is hot, do not rely entirely on the air-conditioning in the vehicle to keep the temperature cool, but place the cichlids so they are out of direct sunlight. The plastic bag will be filled mainly with air rather than water, and must be kept the right way up, being firmly positioned so that it cannot topple over. The plastic bag is usually enclosed in a brown bag as well, to darken the environment and make the journey less stressful for the cichlids.

Everything should be prepared in advance, so that when you arrive home, you simply need to float the plastic bag in the aquarium. Leave it here for 15 minutes or so, to allow the temperature within the bag to equilibrate gradually with that of the aquarium water. You can then net the cichlids carefully, releasing them into their new quarters. It will help them to settle down if you do not put the aquarium lighting on immediately. Wait a day. Similarly, the cichlids are unlikely to feed avidly when first introduced to their new quarters, so only offer a little food over the course of the first 24 hours, since it is likely to be ignored and will then end up polluting the tank.

CLASSIFICATION

The classification of cichlids is often a controversial area, with numerous changes being made over the years. It is possible that many of the taxonomic arguments may be settled through DNA investigations in the future, but at present, various species can be found in the literature under different names. This can lead to confusion, especially where the previous scientific description has been incorporated into the common name for the species, as has happened with haplochromis. The haplochromis goldfin is now known scientifically as *Copadichromis borleyi*.

The classification process operates through a series of ranks, which become progressively more specific, narrowing down to enable individual populations to be identified. This works as follows:

Kingdom: Animalia
Phylum: Chordata
Class: Actinopterygii
Order: Perchiformes
Family: Cichlidae
Tribe: Tropheini
Genus: *Tropheus*
Species: *Tropheus duboisi*

DEFINITION OF THE CICHLID FAMILY	
Phylum Chordata:	vertebrates
Subphylum Vertebrata:	animals with vertebral column
Superclass Gnathostomata:	jawed fish
Grade Teleostomi:	bony fish
Class Actinopterygii:	ray-finned fish
Subclass Neopterygii	
Division Teleosti:	modern bony fish
Superorder Acanthopterygii:	spiny-rayed fish
Order Perchiformes	
Suborder Labroidei	
Family Cichlidae	
(And taxonomists don't even agree about this!)	

Below the level of species, it may be possible to distinguish further individual populations or races. There are three in this particular case for *Tropheus duboisi*, named after the areas where they originate around Lake Tanganyika—Bemba, Kigoma, and Malagarazi.

Ranks at the level of genus or below are written in italics, giving a useful indicator about where one is within the taxonomic tree. The scientific study of fish, known as ichthyology, relies on a number of physical characteristics when ascribing species to different genera, such as the appearance and number of scales plus the shape of the teeth, as well as more evident features like body profile, although coloration is of less significance. A new species can only be given a name when it has been described in the scientific literature.

There are many cichlid candidates for life in the home aquarium, and the following breakdown (based on their geographic origins) gives an indication of the most widely kept genera. Individual fish do differ in terms of their temperament, however, so that guidelines in this respect are not infallible.

AMERICAN CICHLIDS

Aequidens

These New World cichlids are quite easy to look after, and not especially demanding in their water chemistry needs. Members of this genus may also sometimes be described as *Acara* species. Those commonly kept in aquariums can vary from approximately 4in (10cm) in the case of Hoehne's nannacara (*A. hoehnei*) up to Michael's cichlid (*A. michaeli*), which may grow to 12in (30cm) in length. Although

◗ The blue acara (*Aequidens pulcher*), one of the most widely kept members of its genus, was first seen in Europe back in 1906.

territorial by nature, pairs are not too aggressive. While typically spawning in the open on rockwork, certain *Aequidens* cichlids such as *A. diadema* subsequently prove to be mouthbrooders, with both members of the pair participating in this activity. They are generally omnivorous in their feeding habits.

Amphilophus

Members of this genus are sometimes combined as part of the *Cichlasoma* genus. Most of these Central American cichlids will require spacious accommodations, with the largest members of the group growing to more than 13in (35cm) in length. As they mature, the male fish develop a characteristic nuchal hump in some cases, such as the midas cichlid (*A. citrinellus*), creating a visible swelling on the forehead. *Amphilophus* cichlids can be aggressive by nature. They will hunt for food in the substrate, and it appears that variations in body size between different populations in the wild are directly influenced by the availability of food. In the case of *A. longimanus*, individuals found in the Pacific drainage systems can reach 7.5in (18cm), which is half as big again as those occurring in the rivers draining into the Caribbean Sea. They tend to be open spawners, although smaller species are more inclined to spawn under the protection of an overhang. Relatively adaptable in terms of water chemistry, these cichlids are omnivorous so feeding them in the aquarium is straightforward.

Apistogramma

These dwarf cichlids have an unusually rounded caudal fin. Males tend to be beautifully colored and are significantly larger in size than females. They typically average about 2.5–3in (6–7.5cm) long, with

⬆ Longfin cichlid (*Amphilophus longimanus*). So-called because of the length of its pelvic fins, this Central American species will dig repeatedly in the substrate. Worms are a favored food.

bigger members of the group such as the Jurua dwarf cichlid (*A. juruensis*) attaining 4in (10cm) in length. Males should be kept in the company of several females. An interesting feature of some members of the group is that the water temperature can affect the sex of the offspring (see page 92). In the case of the panda dwarf cichlid (*A. nijsseni*), females only will arise in a low temperature band of 68–73°F (20–23°C), with exclusively male fish occurring at a water temperature above 84.4°F (29.1°C). Between these figures, fry of both sexes will result. Soft, acid water is very important for these cichlids, whose diet should include live food on a regular basis.

➲ Panda dwarf cichlid (*Apistogramma nijsseni*). An immediately recognizable feature is the rounded caudal fin of most males. In other *Apistogramma* species there are usually upper and lower fin-ray extensions.

Archocentrus

The convict cichlid (*A. nigrofasciatum*) is the best-known member of this genus, which comprises species that have previously featured in the *Cichlasoma* genus. They are medium-sized, with the largest of these Central America cichlids being *A. centrarchus*, males of which grow to 6in (15cm) overall, with females being slightly smaller. Relatively hardy, territorial, and potentially aggressive, these cichlids are easy to care for, and will often breed in aquarium surroundings. They are cave spawners, with clay pots being adopted readily as substitute spawning sites. Pairs usually prove to be devoted parents. They thrive on an omnivorous diet, which includes *Spirulina* or a similar substitute for the algae that they browse on in the wild.

Astronotus

Although the oscar (*A. ocellatus*) is the best-known member of this genus, a number of other cichlids are sometimes incorporated into

this genus, like the black belt cichlid (*A. parma*). The confused state of cichlid taxonomy is such that this particular fish is also considered by some to be grouped in the genera *Cichlasoma*, *Astatheros*, *Chuco*, and *Heros*. This also applies in the case of other *Astronotus* species. They all tend to be relatively large cichlids, typically growing up to 12in (30cm) or so, occurring in parts of both Central and South America. Males may be more brightly colored and have pointed genital papillae, as well as displaying signs of a cephalic hump. They spawn in the open on a suitable substrate and the wrigglers are housed in pits at first. Omnivorous, these cichlids may inflict serious damage on plants in their aquarium by nibbling at them.

○ Flier cichlid (*Archocentrus centrarchus*) from Central America is primarily insectivorous in the wild.

○ This is the so-called red tiger variant of the oscar (*Astronotus ocellatus*).

Cichlasoma

Recent taxonomic changes have led to the splitting of what was formerly the extensive *Cichlasoma* genus, in which many New World cichlids were grouped together, into a number of separate genera. Just to add to the confusion, the brown acara, now recognized as *C. portalegrensis*, is still sometimes considered as a member of the genus *Aequidens*. It is one of the more southerly *Cichlasoma* representatives,

● Port cichlid (*Cichlasoma portalegrensis*). Also sometimes described as the brown cichlid or brown acara because of its coloration.

being present in parts of Argentina, Bolivia, and Paraguay, so that along with the Bolivian cichlasoma (*C. boliviense*), for example, it does not require such a high water temperature as species originating closer to the Equator. A typical range of 72–77°F (22–25°C) will suit these particular omnivorous fish. They are of medium size, growing to about 5in (13cm) overall, and spawn in the open.

Geophagus

The generic name of these cichlids translates literally as "earth eaters," which is a reflection of the fact that members of this group dig avidly in search of edible items in the substrate. This means they can be very disruptive to plants in their aquarium, although they are relatively unfussy about water conditions. As in other cases, there have been revisions to their taxonomy, to the extent that some members of the *Geophagus* group have now been split off into different genera, such as *Gymnogeophagus*. These cichlids are unusual among New World species in that some have evolved forms of mouthbrooding behavior. Typically, a pair will spawn on a cleaned area of smooth rockwork. However, in some species, such as the pearl cichlid (*G. brasiliensis*), the female then collects up the eggs in her mouth, retaining them here until the fry hatch about three weeks later. In

● Banded cichlid (*Heros severus*). This is an example of the golden variety, which is more brightly colored than the wild form.

other cases, the male may assist his partner, with the eggs being left on the rock where they were laid until just before they hatch, then being taken into the mouths of the adult fish. This is sometimes described as "delayed mouthbrooding" behavior.

Heros

This generic name has been considered to be synonymous with *Cichlasoma* in some cases. Unfortunately, it is not just the generic name that changes; *H. angulifer*, for example, is now considered to be the same as *C. intermedia*, while *H. deppii* corresponds to *C. sieboldii*. Males are generally larger than females, and territorial by nature, becoming more aggressive during the breeding period. They are easy to maintain on a varied diet, incorporating live food, and they spawn in the open on a suitable piece of rock. Both parents share in the task of protecting their offspring. Water conditions can be between soft and medium-hard, with a pH reading of about neutral required. Members of this group have been represented in aquariums for over a century, and they can be maintained successfully without great difficulty.

⬆ Pearl cichlid (*Geophagus brasiliensis*). Keen diggers, these cichlids will regularly burrow around in the aquarium substrate.

Microgeophagus

The two colorful species comprising this genus—Ramirez's dwarf cichlid (*M. ramirezi*) and the Bolivian butterfly cichlid (*M. altispinosa*)—were formerly classified within the *Apistogramma* grouping. Their revised generic name reflects their association with *Geophagus* as well as their smaller size. They typically grow to about 3in (7.5cm) in length, which makes them ideal for smaller aquariums. Pairs will spawn on flat rocks, with females tending to guard the eggs while males maintain their territorial boundaries, becoming more assertive at this stage. Both then protect their offspring once they are transferred to spawning pits. *Microgeophagus* cichlids are likely to be seen at their best in soft, slightly acid water, with regular water changes being especially important as they are adversely affected by any accumulation of nitrogenous waste in their aquarium.

Nandopsis

These large and often strikingly patterned cichlids are to be found in parts of both Central and South America, growing up to 20in (50cm) in the case of the tiger cichlid (*N. festae*). In comparison, males of Mia's cichlid (*N. vombergae*), one of the smallest members of the genus kept in the aquarium, reach a maximum size of about 8in (20cm). Females in all cases are slightly smaller. Unfortunately, *Nandopsis* cichlids are highly belligerent and so it is not possible to house them in groups. Most species will prove to be disruptive to plants, with the possible exception of Salvin's cichlid (*N. salvini*).

⬇ Bolivian butterfly cichlid (*Microgeophagus altispinosa*). Males can be easily distinguished by their brighter coloration.

Pterophyllum

This genus comprises the popular angelfish, with their tall, slender striped bodies. There is considerable dispute about the taxonomy of these cichlids, however, and the relationship between the different species. Some consider the long-nosed angelfish (*P. dumerilii*), found in the lower reaches of the Amazon, as being separate from *P. scalare*. It has a prominent black spot on each side of the body below the dorsal fin, and a more elongated appearance overall. This is due to the slope of the head, which is not as rounded as in other angelfish and explains its alternate common name of sheepshead angel. Pairs make very graceful tank occupants, while young fish can be kept in schools. Inhabiting stretches of calm water, these cichlids do not like strong currents in their aquarium, so site any power filter carefully, to avoid disruption.

Satanoperca

Another genus created from species formerly incorporated into the *Geophagus* grouping, these cichlids are typically encountered in sandy stretches of water and will dig regularly in the aquarium substrate. They are not especially aggressive fish however, in spite of typically averaging 8–11in (20–28cm) in length, but pairs do require suitably spacious surroundings. Originating relatively close to the equator, they require warm surroundings, at a water temperature of about 81°F (27°C). Omnivorous, live food should figure regularly in their diet, and may help to encourage spawning. While *Satanoperca* cichlids spawn in the open, some appear to be delayed mouthbrooders, in common with a number of *Geophagus* species, as females collect their eggs up from their spawning sites about a day or so after laying occurs.

🡡 Jack Dempsey cichlid (*Nandopsis octofasciatus*). Attractive and easy to keep, but aggressive and will dig in the aquarium substrate.

↑ Angelfish
(*Pterophyllum scalare*)
are instantly
recognizable.

➲ Right, top: Three-
spot eartheater (*Satan-
operca daemon*) has
proved difficult to
spawn successfully.
Right, middle: Discus
(*Symphysodon aequi-
fasciatus*) now exist
in a wide range of
domesticated strains.
Right, bottom:
Firemouth cichlids
(*Thorichthys meeki*).

Symphysodon

Discus have become one of the most popular of all cichlids, being widely bred around the globe, in spite of the fact that they can also rank among the most expensive, certainly in the case of some of the rarer color forms. Water quality is vital for the successful mainte-nance of these fish. Otherwise, they are prone to developing envi-ronmentally linked illnesses such as hole-in-the-head disease. The so-called Heckel discus (*S. discus*) can be distinguished from the dis-cus (*S. aequifasciatus*) itself by the presence of a much broader dark vertical band which extends from the base of the dorsal fin down each side of the body to the anal fin. In the case of *S. aequifasciatus*, all the bands are of roughly equal width. It does seem likely, howev-er that these two species hybridize naturally in the wild, where their distributions overlap.

Thorichthys

These medium-sized cichlids found in Central America typically aver-age around 6in (15cm) when adult. Males are more brightly colored, often having reddish-orange underparts. One of the behavioral

⊃ The window or mosaic cichlid (*Vieja fenestratus*). This is one of the larger members of the genus.

⊃ Black belt cichlid (*Vieja maculicauda*). A popular species, so-called because of its broad body stripe, although this characteristic can vary in extent between individuals.

⊃ The two-striped or red-spotted cichlid (*Vieja bifasciatus*). These Central American cichlids are likely to eat plants included in their aquarium.

differences that sets this genus of cichlids apart from *Amphilopus* is that they are able to feed in shallow water, and not just because of their smaller size. They also adopt a more horizontal feeding posture, as they search the substrate for edible items. Snails feature in the diets of some species, and such invertebrates are likely to fall victim to them in aquarium surroundings. Pair-bonding only occurs during the immediate spawning period. The eggs are laid typically on rockwork in the open, with the young wrigglers then being moved to a pit which has already been dug in the substrate nearby, when they emerge about two days later. It is then quite usual for the fry to be moved again until they are free-swimming.

Vieja

Represented both in Central and South America, these large cichlids are often multi-colored. Males invariably grow larger than females, typically reaching 12–16in (30–40cm). Members of this group have previously been incorporated into other genera, including *Cichlasoma*, *Heros,* and *Theraps.* They are primarily herbivorous, especially when older, and therefore likely to destroy plants in their aquarium. Egg laying takes place on rockwork, which is cleaned by both parents beforehand. Their large size means that compatibility can be a particular problem—greatest success is likely to be achieved if immature fish are allowed to pair off on their own, and then housed separately. *Vieja* species are relatively undemanding about water chemistry, but a good filtration system to maintain water quality, along with regular water changes, is vital to their well-being.

OLD WORLD AFRICAN & ASIATIC CICHLIDS

Altolamprologus

The greater body width of these Lake Tanganyikan cichlids, combined with the height of their dorsal fin, distinguishes them from *Neolamprologus* species. Males grow significantly larger than females, to a maximum length of about 6in (15cm). *Altolamprologus* cichlids inhabit sandy areas of the lake, where they breed in snail shells, so their aquarium should be planned accordingly. The male fertilizes the eggs from outside the shell, so it should be too small for him to enter, and then patrols the surrounding area, driving off any possible intruders. These cichlids are not social by nature with others of their own kind, and so need to be housed in individual pairs. They have been known to eat the eggs of mouthbrooding species on occasion, although their natural diet is based mainly on live foods. Water conditions should be hard and alkaline, with a pH between 7.5 and 9.5, while the temperature should be between 73–81°F (23–27°C).

⊕ Pearly lamprologus (*Altolamprologus calvus*). This genus is endemic to Lake Tanganyika.

Aulonocara

This genus of Lake Malawian cichlids typically range in size from about 3–8in (8.5–20cm) in the case of males in their native habitat, but they tend to grow larger in aquarium surroundings. Females can usually be identified by their small size, and tend to be less colorful, particularly when compared with males in breeding condition. Accurate identification can be problematic in some cases, because *Aulonocara* species often have localized distribution, and occur in various forms, which means that individuals can differ quite widely in appearance. Their accommodation needs do not differ significantly from those of other Rift Valley cichlids. Males are likely to be aggressive toward others of their own kind, but usefully for the aquarist, are rather more tolerant with different species.

⊕ Yellow regal cichlid (*Aulonocara baenschi*). Some morphs can be confused with *Haplochromis* species.

Copadichromis

These haplochromis cichlids are widely distributed through Lake Malawi, with some species such as *Copadichromis quadrimaculatus mbarule* migrating around the lake on occasions, seeking new feeding grounds. Males average 4–8in (10–20cm) in length and are highly territorial by nature, with females being smaller and living in schools, along with

young fish. As part of their courtship, some males will construct semicircular sandcastles, that attract females when they are ready to spawn. After mating, the female collects her eggs in her mouth, hatching and caring for the young on her own. While some species occur in sandy parts of the lake however, others are found in more rocky areas, and this needs to be reflected in their aquarium surroundings. Not all the species that are available have received scientific names as yet, and so these are simply known under various trade descriptions, which may indicate the part of the lake where they are found.

⬆ Nguwa (*Copadichromis chrysonotus*). This species is also sometimes described scientifically as *C. jacksoni*, and as *Haplochromis jacksoni*.

Cyprichromis

Members of this genus, occurring in Lake Tanganyika, are quite active by nature, as is apparent from their streamlined appearance, and their aquarium must incorporate adequate open areas for swimming. In the wild, they are often encountered in large schools, frequently swimming close to rocky outcrops. They are not especially aggressive in aquarium surroundings and can be kept in groups, although occasionally males may prove belligerent toward each other. Most species average between 4–5in (10–12.5cm). Their mouths are surprisingly flexible, enabling them to feed easily on plankton, which they frequently do, with their heads directed downward, even swimming completely upside down in some cases. Although mouthbrooders, they are unusual because females spawn close to the surface, using their mouths to grab eggs as they sink. They show relatively little interest in their offspring once they have hatched, about three weeks later.

⊕ Slender-bodied blue flash (*Cypri-chromis leptosoma*).

⊕ Malawi blue dolphin (*Cyrtocara moorii*). They follow other species that shift sand, darting in to obtain disturbed morsels.

Cyrtocara

The taxonomy of this large group of cichlids originating from Lake Malawi is confused. The majority of members of this genus split into some 20 different genera. Actual identification can therefore be difficult, owing to localized variants, and indeed, not all known species have been exported in any event. Many display blue coloration, such as the Malawi blue dolphin, so called because of its facial shape, with males developing a nuchal hump on the top of their heads as they mature. These cichlids typically reach sizes of 6–10in (15–25cm), with males in general larger than their mates. Breeding behavior differs, with some males being much more territorial than others. Females are mouthbrooders. They require a varied diet, and water conditions as for other Lake Malawi cichlids.

Haplochromis

Many of the species formerly classified in the *Haplochromis* genus have been reclassified as *Cyrtocara* species, originating from Lake Malawi. In addition, *Haplochromis* cichlids are also recognized from the Lake Victoria basin (for example, *H. limax* originates from Lakes George and Edward) as well as the connecting Kazinga Channel. Overall, relatively few of these species from the Victorian group of lakes are widely known in aquarist circles. They are mouthbrooders, with males having particularly striking eggspots on their anal fins to attract the females here. These are relatively small cichlids, averaging about 4in (10cm) in most cases, and an aquarium

housing them should incorporate adequate rockwork retreats, where females can dart back if they feel threatened.

Hemichromis

These river-dwelling cichlids occur in West Africa, being popularly described as jewel fish on account of their beautiful coloration, especially the male fish. Shades of red often predominate, with a blackish blotch behind the eyes. There may be other dark markings elsewhere on their bodies too. Members of this genus, numbering up to 11 recognized species, require very different water conditions from the lake-dwelling African cichlids, as they inhabit streams swollen with rain, often flowing through forested areas. Soft, acidic

⬆ Top: *Haplochromis* species. Many of these cichlids, including this individual, have yet to be officially classified, and so they may only have a "trade name."

⬆ Above: Red jewel cichlid (*Hemichromis bimaculatus*).

water conditions are therefore essential for these cichlids, which grow to about 4–6in (10–15cm) in length. Some species are more aggressive than others, and pairs should ideally be kept apart from other fish when spawning. This usually takes place on a rock, with the young cichlids being transferred to a spawning pit after hatching.

Julidochromis

One of the characteristics that sets these cichlids apart from others found in the Rift Valley lakes is that they are not mouthbrooders. Instead, they spawn in a cave, laying green eggs, and both members of the pair subsequently help to care for the fry. Popularly known as julies, members of this genus are confined to Lake Tanganyika. A rounded caudal fin and a long yet narrow dorsal fin are general characteristics of *Julidochromis* species, with a number of these cichlids displaying striped patterning. They are not social by nature, although in the aquarium it is possible to keep a male in the company of several females, forming a harem. Rockwork should feature prominently in their aquarium, providing both retreats as well as potential spawning sites.

Labeotropheus

These two species of Malawian cichlid vary greatly in appearance. They range widely through the lake, although their populations are often isolated. Not all of the color morphs that are now recognized occur in the wild—some have arisen thanks to breeding in aquariums. Blue coloration predominates, although orange variants are not uncommon. They occur at different depths and feed by grazing on the algal mats, called aufwuchs, which are tightly bound to the rocks.

The slightly larger *L. fuelleborni* occurs in shallower surroundings than *L. trewavasae*, although the natural range of male size is 4–9in (10–18cm) depending on lake locality. This is a direct result of variations in the availability of food. Males are highly territorial, especially when confronted by other males, as they defend the caves where females are attracted to spawn. The eggs are fertilized in the female's mouth.

⬆ Once the scientific name is confirmed, there can still often be confusion about the common name, as with *Julidochromis regani*, known as either striped or Regan's julie. This is another of the Lake Tanganyikan cichlids occurring in several distinctive color morphs.

Lamprologus

These cichlids are widely distributed through Lake Tanganyika, but it is the smaller species averaging 2–3in (5–7.5cm) in length that attract greatest interest among aquarists, because of their breeding habits. They inhabit sandy areas, and their housing should be planned accordingly: As for other Rift Valley cichlids, the water must be medium-hard and alkaline. The water temperature itself ought to be quite low, typically 73–77°F (23–25°C). Snail shells should be strategically positioned for breeding purposes over the floor.

⊕ Fuelleborn's cichlid (*Labeotropheus fuelleborni*). The eggs may be laid in a cave or on a flat rock, before being collected up by the female in her mouth.

⊖ Golden lamprologus (*Lamprologus ocellatus*). Both members of the pair will guard the eggs and then the fry. Live foods should feature prominently in the diet of these small cichlids.

Although these cichlids are territorial, they only defend a small area immediately around the chosen breeding site. Brine shrimp nauplii are important for successful rearing of the fry, and will be eaten by the adult fish as well, which typically feed on plankton in the wild. Larger *Lamprologus* species such as *L. lemairii* prove to be substrate spawners however, seeking the security of caves for this purpose, and cannot be mixed with their smaller counterparts as they are piscivorous.

Melanochromis

Members of this genus, originating from Lake Malawi often go by the common name of mbuna, being rock dwellers, feeding on the algae growing in these areas of the lake. The typical size range is 3–6in (7.5–15cm) or so, with females usually slightly smaller in size than males. In some cases, there is also marked sexual dimorphism, with females differing in coloration from males. This is particularly evident in the exotically named pearl of Likoma (*M. joanjohnsoni*), named after the island of Likoma around which these cichlids are found. Just to complicate the position, there are also various localized populations that differ from each other in their coloration. Their care corresponds to that of other herbivorous cichlids from the Rift Valley lakes, with females being mouthbrooders.

⊕ Pearl of Likoma (*Melanochromis joanjohnsoni*). The sexes differ widely in appearance in this species. The male seen here has a prominent black stripe running across the dorsal fin that is absent in the female.

Neolamprologus

This relatively large genus features cichlids that differ widely in their habits. Some of the smallest are the peaceful, snail-dwelling species such as multifasciatus big eye (*N. similis*). This species is found in the southern half of Lake Tanganyika and grows to about 1.5in (4cm). Larger, more aggressive *Neolamprologus* cichlids, such

↑ The fairy cichlid
(*Neolamprologus
brichardi*) occurs along
the rocky shoreline
of Lake Tanganyika.
It is also sometimes
called the lyretail
lamprologus.

as the pearl-lined lamprologus (*N. tetracanthus*) may attain a length of 8in (20cm). One of the most popular members of this genus is the fairy cichlid (*N. brichardi*), which is unusual in its behavior, as these fish live well in schools. For breeding purposes however, pairs should have separate cavelike areas available to them. Males are recognizable by the longer tips on their dorsal and caudal fins. This is one of the species where older young will help their parents to defend newly hatched fry, acting as helpers.

The most colorful *Neolamprologus* species is the lemon cichlid (*N. leleupi*), although some individuals are of a more brownish shade. Their coloration is derived in part from their diet, and offering foods high in carotene to aquarium fish will maintain their bright coloration. Brine shrimp should be used for rearing fry partly for this reason. Adult fish will eat a variety of foodstuffs in the aquarium, although they prefer live foods.

Nimbichromis

These Lake Malawian cichlids typically average 9–10in (22.5–25cm) in length, and all are predatory in their feeding habits. Some prove to be more active hunters than others, with *N. livingstonii* being an ambush predator, seizing any scavengers that come within reach of its supposedly dead body. Territorial by nature, especially when breeding, *Nimbichromis* can be maintained on prepared diets, although they prefer live foods. Males are usually more colorful, and have more elaborate fins. After spawning, the female will brood the eggs in her mouth until they hatch, and watches over the young for a further

period. Some *Nimbochromis* cichlids will burrow into the substrate on a regular basis, which can make it difficult to establish plants in an aquarium housing these fish.

Pelvicachromis

Members of this West African genus of cichlids are often described as kribs, and tend to be brightly colored, which has helped to ensure their popularity among aquarists. They typically average about 4in (10cm) overall, with females tending to be smaller in size. Their coloration in the wild is quite variable, with a number of different color morphs having been described, some of which have also become

⬆ Yellow kribs (*Pelvicachromis humilis*). The yellow coloration is only seen in male fish. Females in contrast have red or violet coloration to their bellies.

well established in aquariums. Pairs are relatively peaceful, although they are likely to become far more territorial during the spawning period. Water conditions differ somewhat, according to the species. Yellow kribs (*P. humilis*), for example, require soft, acidic water whereas eyespot kribs (*P. subocellatus*) will benefit from medium hard, slightly acidic surroundings, and the addition of a little marine salt to create the brackish water conditions in which they normally live. Kribs generally spawn within the confines of a suitable cave, with a clay pot sufficing for this purpose in an aquarium. Both the eggs and subsequently the fry are guarded for a time by their parents.

Pseudotropheus

Originating from Lake Malawi, these mbuna cichlids tend to have quite localized distributions, and their taxonomy is often contentious. A number of species occur in different color morphs, with blue, orange, and yellow coloration predominant. They typically average 4–5in (10–12.5cm) in length, with males proving to be territorial and aggressive. Much still remains to be learned about the habits of individual species. The hornet cichlid (*P. crabro*), for example, is often found in close association with the catfish (*Bagrus meridionalis*), keeping the larger fish's body free of parasites. However, it has its own more sinister motivation for this act of charity, in that it preys both on the eggs of the catfish and its fry. *Pseudotropheus* cichlids are mouthbrooders, the eggs being fertilized as the female nibbles at the male's eggspots. After the eggs hatch, she will continue watching over the fry for several days. Adults will take a range of foods, but prefer live foods.

⊖ Polystigma (*Nimbichromis polystigma*). These cichlids must not be mixed with smaller companions that would ultimately be eaten by them.

Protomelas

Not all members of this genus, occurring in Lake Malawi, have yet been ascribed scientific names. They are relatively large cichlids, typically 6–10in (15–25cm) in size. Although displaying territorial instincts when spawning, they are relatively peaceful at other times. Some, such as fenestratus (*P. fenestratus*), are found close to the shoreline, and their rocky habitat, mixed with some open sandy areas, must be reflected in their aquarium surroundings. Sexing is usually straightforward on the basis that male fish are much more brightly colored than females. A single male should be accommodated

⊕ Hornet cichlid (*Pseudotropheus crabro*). The brown and yellow coloration of these fish is responsible for their common name, rather than their aggression.

Moorii (*Tropheus moorii*). These cichlids are widely distributed through the southern part of Lake Tanganyika, occurring in many different forms, including the yellow-banded seen here.

with several females in an aquarium for breeding purposes. Females brood the eggs in their mouths and look after the young when they first hatch. Although not difficult to feed, these cichlids will display a strong preference for live food, which can also act as a spawning trigger.

Tropheus

Members of this mouthbrooding genus are very popular aquarium occupants. They originate from Lake Tanganyika, where they feed on the algae growing on rocks. These species need a corresponding herbivorous diet in an aquarium, which can include fresh algae and greenstuff. *Tropheus* cichlids average 5–6in (13–15cm) in length, and although they do display some territorial instincts, they are not too

aggressive, if a male is housed in the company of several females. The white-spotted cichlid (*T. duboisi*) is generally regarded as the most tolerant member of the genus. Rockwork must be incorporated into the aquarium, providing retreats for these fish. Spawning occurs in the open, with the female then gathering up her eggs at once. A bulge in the vicinity of the throat is usually an indicator that spawning has occurred, rather than being indicative of any health problem. The female will ignore food throughout the incubation period, which may last for three to four weeks (*see also* pages 19-20).

◉ Fenestratus (*Protomelas fenestratus*). This particular species is also sometimes known as *Haplochomis steveni* "Thick Bars"— obviously a reference to the dark barring on the sides of its body.

Etroplus

The two members of this Asiatic genus of cichlids, known as chromides, are often encountered in brackish waters and these conditions can be easily replicated in the aquarium by the addition of marine salt to the water here. Typically allow approximately 2–3 tablespoons per 2.5gal (10l), although the aim should be to replicate the existing water conditions under which the cichlids were being kept at the time of purchase, to minimize the stress of a move. The water chemistry needs to be hard and alkaline, with the temperature 79–82°F (26–28°C). While the orange chromide is unlikely to exceed 3in (7.5cm) in length, its green relative (*E. suratensis*) can grow much larger, up to 18in (45cm) in the wild. Visual sexing of these fish is difficult, but females may be slightly duller in color than males. Pairs become more territorial at spawning time, with egg-laying often occurring on rockwork. The adult cichlids will watch over their brood, placing them in a spawning pit at first, before they start to become free-swimming at a week old.

◉ Green chromide (*Etroplus suratensis*). This species is less conveniently housed than its orange relative (*E. maculatus*) because of its much larger size.

CHAPTER 3

Characteristics and Care

Most cichlids are not suitable for a mixed community aquarium. This is either because they grow to a large size and are likely to prey upon smaller companions, or simply because their water chemistry requirements are specialized. Nevertheless, cichlids are not difficult fish to house in a home aquarium.

THE RIGHT TANK

Young cichlids grow relatively quickly, and so it is likely to be false economy to obtain a small setup at the outset, only to have to replace it within a few months. Choose a tank and filtration system that will be able to meet your needs for the foreseeable future. As a guide to the likely size of accommodation which the cichlids will need, allow roughly 1 gallon per inch (1.5–2l/2.5cm) of their adult size.

Allowing even more space will lessen the likelihood of aggressive encounters, which can occur during the spawning period if cichlids are overcrowded. A well-planted, larger aquarium gives a female

⚠ SIZE MATTERS

It is important to choose species carefully, with a view to their long-term housing. Bear in mind, for example, that the small oscars (*Astronotus ocellatus*) for sale in aquatic stores can ultimately grow to over 1ft (30cm) in length, and will need extra space accordingly. In addition, the feeding habits of these fish mean that there must be a very efficient filtration system in place as well, to safeguard their welfare.

➔ Albino tiger oscar
(*Astronotus ocellatus* var.).

more chance to avoid being harried by a male who is eager to mate. There will also be more possible spawning sites, increasing the likelihood of breeding success. This is important because some cichlids can be very particular about where they lay their eggs.

There are other advantages in having a larger tank. Bigger cichlids can be quite destructive and by providing them with a large tank you can prevent widescale uprooting of plants. Even if you have chosen smaller cichlids, a relatively large tank may allow you to set up a mixed tank of African Rift Valley cichlids, for example. Remember, though, that you should not include closely related species since there is a risk of hybridization. Cichlids display varying degrees of parental care for their offspring, so a large aquarium also provides space for young fish to remain with the adults. Watching them together in these surroundings will give you a fascinating insight into one of the most remarkable aspects of the biology and behavior of these fish.

If your space is limited, some species can be housed in aquariums that are just 24in (61cm) in length. The dwarf Egyptian mouth-brooder (*Pseudocrenilabrus multicolor*), for example, only attains a maximum length of 3in (7.5cm). The height of the aquarium is less significant than its length, except in the case of tall-bodied cichlids such as the angelfish (*Pterophyllum* spp.), where a depth of about 18in (45cm) is recommended. The width of the tank can be an issue too: Larger cichlids must obviously be able to turn round easily, as they swim up and down their quarters.

◑ It is vital to set up an aquarium that meets the particular requirements of the cichlids that you intend to keep. An Amazonian setup is shown here, with plants that will thrive in the requisite soft, acidic water conditions.

Aquarium material

Aquariums today are manufactured from either glass or acrylic. Acrylic tanks are becoming more popular again, although these tend to be sold as complete units, with a matching hood and all the necessary equipment such as a heaterstat and filter unit. They are lighter to handle than glass, and probably less susceptible to being damaged by careless handling, although they can crack if dropped. Their sides are easily scratched, however. This is an important consideration, especially in the case of herbivorous Rift Valley cichlids. These fish need relatively high lighting levels to trigger algal growth, supplementing their diet. This also necessitates cleaning the front of the aquarium frequently, to prevent it becoming obscured by colonies of these microscopic plants. Any scratches are likely to be highlighted, as algae will multiply in these depressions. Here they will be hard to remove, spoiling the appearance of the aquarium as a result.

Glass, on the other hand, can be cleaned with a scraper with no serious risk of damage, although it too has some drawbacks. Large tanks are heavy and cumbersome, requiring two people to carry them safely. A secure base will be vital to take their weight. In addition, even once in position, they can be damaged by large cichlids, which may dislodge rockwork, causing this to smash against the side of the aquarium.

Today's glass tanks are generally held together using special silicone sealant, which absorbs the force of the water rather than creating a rigid bond. When buying any tank of this type, always check the sealant is adequately distributed around the interior. Sometimes, especially in the corners of tanks, the bond may not be complete and there is a risk of leakage. It is also important to check all four of the lower corners, because it is here that glass is most likely to be damaged in transit, if the tank is carelessly handled. Damage of this type may not be immediately obvious, as the fragments of glass often become compressed, rather than actually breaking away.

Choosing the location

You will need to decide at the outset where you want to site the aquarium. Once it is full of water, it will be virtually impossible to move without being emptied again. This process, apart from being time-consuming for you, will also be very stressful for the fish themselves. Although cichlids come from tropical regions, they should not be positioned in such a way that their tank is in direct sunlight for any length of time, especially around midday. This could cause the water temperature to rise to an excessively high level, and will also stimulate unwanted algal growth.

Each gallon of water weighs 8lb (with a liter weighing 1kg) so a secure base will be essential. While smaller tanks can be positioned on a chest or similar piece of furniture, bigger setups will require a stand, or even a cabinet. For large aquariums, a cabinet is the best option. For one thing, it allows attractive viewing of the cichlids, blending in as a piece of furniture in the room. More significantly, its base can accommodate a filtration system capable of maintaining water quality in a large tank. Cabinets themselves are available in a wide range of styles, both contemporary and traditional, so that it should not be too difficult to find one that blends in well with the style of your home.

THE AQUARIUM FLOOR

The choice of floor covering is very significant for cichlids, both in terms of their biology and also their water chemistry requirements, which vary significantly between different groups. Although a number of artificially colored gravels are now available, these are not

READY-MADE SETUP

You may be able to buy an existing aquarium setup with cichlids already present. Even so, you will need to empty most if not all of the water, because it will be too heavy to move. Any rockwork should be transported separately, with the tank being stripped down, leaving just gravel in the base. It will be useful to bale out the "mature" water into a clean pail if the trip home is relatively short. You can use this water to refill the tank, although the fish themselves should be transported separately (see page 30).

ideal for many cichlids, because they tend to drain the color from the fish. Red gravel, for example, will significantly deaden any similar color, including shades of orange. With color varieties of cichlids that exist as aquarium strains rather than in the wild, white gravel can create a pleasing effect. Obviously, though, this does not create a natural backdrop for the fish.

There are other risks in having an unnaturally bright substrate. Cone cells in the retinas of cichlid eyes allow them to distinguish between colors. Some cichlids, such as discus (*Symphysodon*) species, normally inhabit dark stretches of water. After being kept above a white or similarly bright substrate, these fish appear less brightly colored than they would be in more natural surroundings.

There is also the risk that dyed gravel will not prove to be color-fast, but will leach dye out into the water, with adverse effects on the fish. Plastic-coated gravel, particles of which look like jelly beans, is not ideal for cichlids that dig over the substrate since the coating can be rubbed off, adding to the waste in the tank.

The way in which the tank is filtered will have some impact on the choice of substrate. Especially in the case of smaller cichlids, an undergravel filtration system is a good idea. It offers a natural way of filtering the water, breaking down the ammonia and other waste excreted by the fish. In this case, the substrate itself serves as the filter bed, with a beneficial population of bacteria developing here. These bacteria require oxygen, and a compacted filter bed cuts off the oxygen for the bacteria and blocks the flow of water drawn through the undergravel filter, with potentially catastrophic consequences for the fish. The gravel itself therefore needs to be relatively coarse, with the particles being a minimum of approximately ⅛in (3–4mm). In order to build up an effective depth of gravel for an undergravel filter, allow about 2lb per gallon (1kg per 4.5l).

Most gravel is inert, meaning that it does not affect the water chemistry, but this is important to check, because for some cichlids, which require soft water, any gravel containing limestone is likely to be harmful. Limestone will gradually dissolve, creating harder water conditions. On the other hand, limestone gravel is ideal for use in Rift Valley cichlid tanks, because of its effects on water chemistry, acting both as a water hardener and as a buffer.

◐ The so-called "pigeon blood" discus (*Symphysodon aequifasciatus*), one of the newer color variants now available, created by breeders in Southeast Asia. Practically any artificially colored substrate will detract from the beauty of this kind of patterning and tone.

The sand option

Gravel is an unsuitable substrate for some species, especially those Rift Valley cichlids that naturally inhabit sandy areas within the lakes. Some fish keepers have resorted to using coral sand instead, but this has a number of drawbacks—some of which can be serious health hazards for the fish. Being a very fine substrate, it will not work very effectively as a filter bed, and being white, its coloration is not ideal.

For most cichlid species, it is better to stick to gravel as a substrate. Unlike the pieces of coral sand, gravel particles have already

① HYGIENE

Always wash the aquarium out before filling it, especially a new tank where fragments of glass might become impaled in the fish's gills in due course. Secondhand tanks, unless occupied by healthy cichlids, should be disinfected using a special aquarium disinfectant to guard against possible infections.

been rounded off by the action of water, representing virtually no danger to a cichlid that digs into the substrate. If the fish does accidentally ingest gravel, it can be spat out quite easily.

Where sand is required as a substrate, then sand sold specifically as children's play sand (not ordinary building sand) is a better alternative to coral sand. It also tends to be darker in color too, which

❶ African butterfly cichlid (*Anomalo-chromis thomasi*) from western Africa. A species that will not burrow into the substrate. These fish should be provided with flat stones as spawning sites.

means that it has less effect on the color of the fish. Such sand is also usually chemically inert, consisting largely of silica, so that if you want to maintain the buffering effect associated with coral sand, you will need to place a layer of limestone gravel below the sand, or rely on limestone rockwork as decor.

ROCKWORK

The choice of rocks is also particularly significant in an aquarium destined to house cichlids. This again is partly because some rocks are soluble, dissolving away slowly in water so that they alter its chemical composition and relative level of acidity or pH. The water

---

ⓘ CORAL SAND HAZARDS

There is danger in using coral sand, particularly in the case of cichlids that dig into the substrate. The fine particles are sharp, resembling tiny pieces of glass. They can easily become lodged in the delicate gill filaments, being drawn in through the mouth as the fish root about in the sand. Worse still, if particles are inadvertently swallowed along with food, they can become lodged in the throat.

❷ Red terror or tiger cichlid (*Nandopsis festae*): an enthusiastic digger.

requirements of cichlids are quite diverse. Those originating from the Amazonian region typically need soft, acid conditions whereas at the other extreme, those from the Rift Valley lakes of Africa will only thrive if the water is hard and alkaline.

Rocks differ in their chemical composition. Some, such as granite and slate, will prove to be insoluble, and so do not affect the water chemistry. Others, such as the tufa rock often used in tanks housing Rift Valley cichlids, will eventually dissolve. Tufa contains calcium carbonate, being described as calciferous as a result. Distinguishing between these two types is quite straightforward, simply by using vinegar, which is a weak acid. If you are in any doubt, then pour this carefully on to a sliver of the rock. If it starts to bubble, this confirms that the rock is calciferous. The acetic acid present in the vinegar reacts with the calcium carbonate. You may have to look closely to see this effect. Avoid using stronger acids, however, as they are dangerous to handle and difficult to dispose of.

Most aquatic stores stock rockwork suitable for the aquarium, which is usually sold by weight. Although it usually appears quite drab in its dry state, richer, brighter shades of red and green appear once it is submerged in water.

Carefully examine the rocks you choose, to see how they will blend alongside each other in the tank: The rockwork is an integral design feature. Turn the pieces around to appreciate them from different angles. The choice of rockwork for the cichlid tank is more than decorative, however, since many of these fish use rocks for spawning purposes. Those that lay their eggs in the open will prefer a relatively flat surface, and slate is recommended for this purpose. If it needs to be cut to the required size, you will need a hammer, chisel and goggles. Avoid any brown-colored pieces since this is, in effect, rust.

All rocks are heavy and will add considerably to the weight of the aquarium. They can be dislodged by large cichlids, which in the worst case may either break the heaterstat, possibly electrocuting themselves too, or smash the sides of the tank. It is not just a matter of a cichlid dislodging a piece of rock by swimming past—some species will tunnel beneath the rock, causing a tall piece to topple over. Therefore never prop pieces of rock on each other, but always make sure they are firmly positioned in the substrate. But bear in mind that debris may accumulate here around them if you are relying on an undergravel filtration system.

 HOLD IT SAFELY IN PLACE

If you need to create anchorage points to give greater stability, as may be necessary with pieces of slate, you can use the same type of silicone sealant as on the tanks themselves. Never use ordinary household sealants because they contain potentially fatal fungicides.

⊕ Rockwork is an
important feature in
the design of many
cichlid aquariums,
providing both shelter
and spawning sites. It
is a prerequisite for
any Lake Tanganyika
setup containing rock
dwellers of the
Neolamprologus or
Julidochromis genera.

Rockwork alternatives

Inert, lightweight alternatives are now available as substitutes for
actual rockwork. Aquariums for Rift Valley cichlid species may also
incorporate tufa rock, which is more commonly sold for marine
tanks. Tufa is exceptionally porous, so it is very difficult to clean
thoroughly before placing it in the aquarium. All rocks should ideally be scrubbed off in a solution of aquarium disinfectant, and
then rinsed thoroughly, before being added to the tank.

Tufa can provide snug retreats for smaller cichlids in particular, but
its rough surfaces and hollow structure mean that it will not be
adopted for spawning. Alternative sites will be needed. For cave-
dwelling cichlids, you can try granite, using slate to form a roof area.
Another possible option is to use a clay pot. These are available in a
wide range of sizes, and can simply be buried in the substrate.
Breaking these pots can be more problematic, as they do not split
neatly into two halves, but provided there is enough room for the
fish beneath, the cut edges can be disguised in the substrate. It is not
necessarily a good idea to use the whole pot, as this will interfere
with the undergravel filter. Never use a pot that might have con-
tained plants because dangerous pesticide residues could be present.

Clay pipes of various diameters can be added at the outset to
persuade cave-spawning cichlids to lay in aquarium surroundings.
As with clay pots, however, these must be new. Also, you should
soak them first in a bucket of ordinary water to lessen the risk of
any contamination and to check that they have no noticeable
effect on the water chemistry.

PLANTS

Living plants can play an important role within the ecology of the aquarium. They utilize the nitrate produced as a result of the nitrogen cycle. In this process, bacterial action converts waste from the fish from toxic ammonia to nitrite, and finally nitrate itself. Although nitrate is far less toxic to fish, a build-up of this chemical in the water can be harmful. Nitrate acts as a fertilizer for plants, so its removal by the plants is beneficial all round. In addition, plants also use carbon dioxide gas when photosynthesizing during the daytime or in light, producing oxygen that the fish can utilize. However, aquarium plants also take up oxygen in the dark.

The choice of aquarium plants is wide, but it helps to choose those found in the cichlids' natural habitat since plants and fish share the same water requirements. The available range is greatest in the case of cichlids inhabiting areas of the Amazon basin, where the water may be relatively slow-flowing and full of weeds. In such environments the vegetation can have a direct influence on the appearance of cichlids, particularly angelfish (*Pterophyllum* spp.), with their tall, narrow bodies. They can swim very effectively through heavily planted areas, with the markings on their bodies providing camouflage. In the aquarium, these fish should be kept alongside tall, narrow-leaved plants such as vallisnerias.

Some cichlids need vegetation instead of rockwork as potential spawning sites. Plants with relatively broad, upright leaves suit this purpose. Plants growing in the substrate can also help to provide retreats if a male fish starts to pursue his partner relentlessly. In addition, vegetation can also greatly enhance the natural appearance of the aquarium.

🔼 Straight vallis (*Vallisneria* species). Vallis, sometimes known as tape grass, can tolerate most aquarium water conditions.

There can be problems with plants, however. Larger cichlids, and particularly all members of the group that dig in the substrate, can uproot aquarium plants. This can prove to be a particular problem in a newly established aquarium, where the plants have not yet taken hold in the substrate. It is therefore a good idea to set them in small pots, which in turn can be buried in the substrate, as they are less likely to be disturbed by the cichlids with this firmer anchor. Growing aquatic plants in this way, rather than trying to allow them to root in the substrate, has a further long-term advantage. It will help to prevent their roots from growing down and blocking off the slits within an undergravel filter, reducing its effectiveness as a result.

Special needs

Whereas cichlids from parts of Central and South American often live in weedy stretches of water, those from the Rift Valley lakes of Africa occur in environments where plants are generally very localized in their distribution. They tend to be confined to areas at the mouths of the rivers flowing into the lakes, where deposited sediment nourishes their growth. Vallisnerias are common in these surroundings. They can survive in the relatively hard, alkaline waters, and can be cultivated accordingly in the aquarium.

Another useful plant for the Rift Valley aquarium is Java fern (*Microsorum pteropus*). It is relatively hardy and can be cultivated in a number of localities other than just in the substrate. You can attach pieces of Java fern to rockwork, using rubber bands to hold them in place until they establish their roots here.

Since many cichlids prefer relatively subdued lighting, you can incorporate floating plants. These diffuse the light filtering down through the water, while utilizing the nitrate in solution. Local water currents can affect the distribution of these particular plants, so they often end up in one part of the aquarium. Should their growth become too widespread over the surface, part of the resulting mat can be easily scooped out with a net. The most widely grown floating plants, such as Java moss (*Vesicularia dubyana*) and duckweed (*Lemna minor*) multiply rapidly. There must be a gap between the top of the aquarium and the water level in order to incorporate floating plants, and reasonable ventilation too, to ensure that they do not dampen off.

You can buy aquarium plants either from local aquatic stores or by mail order. In either case, it is important that they are not allowed to dry out, and should never be kept out of the water any longer than strictly necessary. Choose plants with healthy green leaves. Draw up a planting scheme for the aquarium, taking into account other design features such as rockwork. With most cichlids, it is usually a

⬆ Natural plants with "keramic" rock decor. Plastic plants do not imply artificial rock, nor do natural rock formations require living vegetation. In the art of the aquarist, there is no law against artfulness.

good idea to place the plants around the sides and toward the back of the aquarium, with an open area for swimming located at the front (*see* diagrams on page 109).

Bogwood is often included in cichlid aquariums where soft, acidic water conditions are required, and is stocked by most aquarist stores. It is quite usual for this material to give the water a distinctive yellowish tint, thanks to the tannin leaching out of it, which is a feature of environments of this type. Bogwood is not just valuable for creating natural water conditions, however—it also provides retreats for the fish and is sometimes chosen by pairs as a spawning site.

THE WATER ITSELF

Creating and maintaining the correct water conditions—vital to the well-being of the cichlids—may depend on your local water supply. For example, you will find it easier to keep Rift Valley cichlids if you live in a hard water area. The hardness of water is a measure of the dissolved mineral salts in it. The Rift Valley lakes contain high amounts because they are relatively stable bodies of water, lacking any major river flows into or out of them.

Rain forms as pure droplets of water in the clouds, but as the raindrops fall they come in contact with carbon dioxide gas in the air, producing carbonic acid. Pollution in the air can also combine with the water. Sulfur dioxide, for example, combines with rain to create a dilute form of sulfuric acid. The rain reaching the ground is therefore slightly acidic.

This acidity may increase still further if the water then flows through decaying vegetation, being exposed to humic acids. If it passes over rocks containing carbonates, this too alters its chemistry, with the salt dissolving into the water, causing it to become hard. Such a chemical change is even greater if the rain percolates down underground through rocks, before returning to the surface as a spring.

Discus (*Symphysodon* spp.) and other cichlids from rivers of South America live in soft, acidic water conditions, so you may need to use reverse osmosis equipment in order to create suitable water conditions for them. In effect, this removes all the dissolved salts, creating pure water which can then be mixed with dechlorinated drinking water, its relative hardness measured previously, to create the appropriate water conditions. In order to achieve this, you will also need a pH buffer. Trace elements are also important—these will have been removed by the reverse osmosis process.

⬆ The addition of aquarium peat to the filtration system will create water conditions similar to those naturally encountered by angelfish (*Pterophyllum* spp.) and other cichlids found in stretches of water in the Amazon region.

Temporary hardness arises from the presence of bicarbonate salts, which can be removed by boiling the water, while permanent hardness is caused by sulfates. These chemicals also affect the degree of acidity as well, so that hard water usually has a correspondingly higher pH than soft water, which is naturally more acidic. The relative degree of acidity is measured on the pH scale, with a pH reading of 7 being neutral: anything above this figure is described as alkaline, while a lower reading is acidic. Monitoring of the pH and relative hardness of water can be carried out quite easily and reliably by means of test kits, sold by aquatic stores, although alternatively LCD-meters will give direct readings from water samples, without the need to use a color chart.

🔾 The triangle cichlid or waru (*Uaru amphiacanthoides*). This is a young fish, as shown by its spots, which are replaced by a streaky patterning in older individuals. Originating from northern South America, these cichlids need soft, acidic water conditions.

The presence of bicarbonates and carbonates in the water helps to neutralize acids, reducing the percentage of hydrogen ions and therefore stabilizing the pH. Unless adequate partial water changes are carried out to replenish the chemical buffers in the aquarium, the pH and hardness in the tank will decline over a period of time. This can be a particular problem in aquariums catering from Rift Valley cichlids, and so the rockwork and other tank decor can be very helpful to maintain the buffering system. Limestone gravel is useful for this purpose, as are larger chunks of calcium-containing rocks, by way of decor. This approach will help to create the necessary more alkaline, higher pH surroundings in an aquarium, bearing in mind that the health of Rift Valley cichlids will be under greater threat from a lower pH than softer water conditions.

TERMS USED TO EXPRESS WATER HARDNESS

0–5 dGH (degrees of general hardness)/0–50 mg/l = very soft
6–9 dGH/50–100 mg/l = moderately soft-soft
10–14 dGH/100–150 mg/l = slightly hard-medium
15–19 dGH/150–200 mg/l = moderately hard
20–28 dGH/200–300 mg/l = hard
Over 28 dGH/over 300 mg/l = very hard

The relative hardness of water is measured in several ways, most widely on the basis of degrees of general hardness scale (dGH), or in terms of mg/l, which is the same as parts per million (ppm). Although rainwater can in theory be used to soften hard water, this option is rarely used, because of the associated risk of pollution. Although fish that have been tank-bred over generations may display more adaptability to different pH and hardness than those from the wild, these distinctions are relative. It can also turn out that commercially bred strains are just as susceptible to health problems unless maintained under ideal water conditions.

The firemouth cichlid (*Thorichthys meeki*) from Central America requires neutral to alkaline, medium-hard water conditions.

POWERED EQUIPMENT

Heaters

In most parts of the world, supplementary heating will be necessary, in order to maintain the correct water temperature within the aquarium. Aquarium heaters are available in different wattages. The choice of heater is influenced not only by the water temperature required in the tank, but also that in the surrounding room. It is generally recommended to work on the basis of allowing 3 watts per gallon (1W per liter). The temperature range required depends

● Most cichlids, like Macmaster's dwarf cichlid (*Apistogramma macmasteri*) shown here, require a water temperature typically in the range of 73–86°F (23–30°C). Though the higher end that this fish can tolerate would be excessive for many other cichlids.

○ Rather than provide photographs of fluorescent tubes, perhaps it is more informative—and certainly more interesting—to consider the natural behavior of these cichlids in Lake Malawi. It is a reminder that natural light is important to provide some cichlids with a food source. These particular fish are feeding on algae on rocks about 20ft (6m) down.

on the species concerned, although generally, Rift Valley cichlids will thrive at slightly lower temperatures than some of the New World species.

Fish can adapt within reason to changes in water temperature, but with new fish, it is important to maintain the temperature at or just slightly higher than what they were used to previously. Their immune systems tend to function more effectively at this level. The traditional way is to rely on a glass heater, which needs to be kept submerged at all times when in operation: It should be left to cool before being lifted out of a tank for any reason. The operating range of the unit is under thermostatic control, and the trend has been to simplify matters, opting for an all-in-one unit, in the guise of a heaterstat, rather than linking the heater to a separate thermostat. Most of the aquarium heaters on the market today come preset, but check that you can adjust the thermostat setting easily if necessary.

This type of heating setup is not necessarily ideal for all cichlids. The behavior of large, more boisterous cichlids can damage a heaterstat unit. In addition, the smooth glass surface of these units means that some fish may be attracted here to spawn, and given the heat output through the glass, their eggs are likely to end up being "fried."

It is not really advisable to screen the heaterstat by placing rockwork around it. This increases the likelihood of localized "hot spots" of water in the tank, and also means that there could be a focus here where mulm is likely to collect, resulting in a deterioration in water quality. It is easier to prevent the use of heaterstats as spawning sites however, simply by using a mesh guard which can be fitted here for this purpose.

Many cichlid keepers now use thin heat pads in diameters matching those of their aquariums. The pads can be fitted under the aquarium, in contact with the base, or on the side. Heat is then transmitted through the glass. They act rather like a radiator heating a room, with the heat output being controlled by a separate thermostat. Moreover, the pads cannot be damaged in any way by the fish.

Lighting

Many aquariums are supplied complete with hoods, which incorporate a sealed lighting unit. It is obviously vital, on safety grounds, to ensure that electrical connections here are not exposed either directly to water, or by the inevitable condensation arising in the aquarium.

The level of sediment in the natural environment of the cichlids influences the amount of light required. Those from Lake Victoria require relatively low levels of lighting, simply because the water in which they occur is often quite murky, thanks to the sediment in solution.

If you notice that your fish appear paler than usual, but otherwise quite lively, it could well be that the level of illumination is too high. It will then be a matter of opting for a lower wattage light, or screening the surface using floating plants to diffuse the level of illumination from above.

Lighting is beneficial, however, in ensuring good algae growth within the aquarium. It provides what is in effect a natural food source for some of these fish: *Tropheus moorii* of Lake Tanganyika,

for example, naturally grazes on algae. Fluorescent tubes, rather than incandescent bulbs, are now used almost universally in aquariums. These emit light rather than heat, in contrast to tungsten bulbs for example, and so will not affect the temperature of the water.

In most cases, the lights will need to be left on for about eight hours per day, in order to ensure maximum benefit, although if you find that algal growth is spreading out of control, one of the steps that you can take to curb it is to shorten the length of time that the lights are left on.

Filtration

The other key piece of electrical equipment required is the filtration system. In an aquarium, fish are housed at much higher densities than would be the case in their natural habitat. Moreover, it is in effect a closed system, with flushing through of the waste products dependent not on rainfall or river flow, but on partial water changes and filtration. An effective filtration system therefore has a vital role to maintain water quality.

Their filtration needs will be influenced not just by their size and stocking density, but also by the waters in which they occur in the wild and their diet. Cichlids differ in their relative susceptibility to nitrogenous compounds, and there are various ways in which the harmful effects of these chemicals can be neutralized by filtration. The value of biological filtration has already been mentioned (see page 61), whereby beneficial bacteria break down the nitrogenous waste as part of the nitrogen cycle.

This is often accomplished by means of an undergravel filter. It is a very simple method, relying on a plastic base plate with holes in it. The base must be placed so it covers the whole floor of the aquarium. The gravel is then placed on top, to a depth of approximately 2in (5cm). It serves as a filter bed, where these bacteria are present. Since they require oxygen, there is a connection between the undergravel filter and an air pump, via the so-called airlift, a tube usually located at the back of the aquarium, where it can be more easily concealed.

It will take time for the bacterial population to multiply here and start to function effectively. This is often described as the maturation period, and can be speeded up by adding a starter culture of these bacteria, either in liquid or powder form. Until this stage is reached, the cichlids are at greater risk of being exposed to fatal levels of ammonia and nitrite.

This type of filter should suit most typical Rift Valley cichlids, which are small and have small appetites but should not be kept at high densities because of their territorial natures. In contrast, cichlids from Central America may inhabit a similarly sparsely vegetated world, where there are few plants to utilize nitrate, but their significantly larger size and feeding habits mean that the water quality can deteriorate rapidly. Worse still, they are not naturally tolerant of any build-up of nitrogenous waste in their aquariums, simply because they naturally inhabit extensive stretches of waters and live at low densities. This means that they require more active water filtration than can be provided by an undergravel system alone.

⬇ Even relatively hardy cichlids such as the convict (*Archocentrus nigrofasciatus*) from Central America will suffer if the water quality in their aquarium is poor.

It is therefore usual to fit a power filter unit in an aquarium housing these cichlids. This consists of various chambers. There is usually a sponge core at the center, where particulate matter is trapped, resulting in what is described as mechanical filtration. Biological filtration also occurs here though, because the sponge also provides a suitable medium which can be colonized by beneficial bacteria. There may also be a charcoal component as well, serving as a chemical filter and actively adsorbing waste. This needs to be used with care, because it will neutralize medication in the water that is intended to be beneficial.

In the case of some cichlid tanks, special aquarium peat may be added to the filter as well. This releases chemicals such as humic acid to maintain the desirable soft, acidic water conditions for species requiring these conditions, like the dwarf South American cichlids

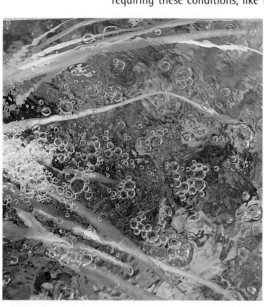

(*Apistogramma* species), fulfilling a similar role to the addition of a blackwater extract within the aquarium itself.

The power filter has its own motor, which sucks water into the unit at a predetermined rate. It is this throughput or turnover that is significant, as larger tanks with greater volumes require correspondingly more powerful filtration units of this type. Internal power filters are suitable for smaller tanks, but for large aquariums, a separate external filter will be needed, drawing water out of the tank and then returning it there after it has passed through the unit. Check on the respective noise level of different units if possi-

↑ It is contact with the air, resulting from movement caused by currents that introduces more oxygen into the water. In the aquarium a power filter assists this process.

ble, because some are louder when operating than others and they need to be left running constantly. The same goes for an undergravel filter and air pump, for which noise considerations may also be significant.

Those designs that, in effect, spray water back into the aquarium have the additional advantage of raising the level of oxygen in the water, by increasing its surface contact with air. All power filters also encourage movement of water around the tank, thanks to the currents that they create.

Even the most effective filtration system does not negate the need to carry out regular partial water changes. Regular monitoring of the water conditions is also vital, especially in the case of a newly established aquarium.

Assembling the components

1. Start by washing off the gravel before placing it in the aquarium. This can be done very easily using a colander, and swirling the

gravel around under a running faucet. Even pre-cleaned gravel is still often dirty and can create a scum on the surface of the water.

2. Put the undergravel filter in place, which should cover the entire floor area of the aquarium, and fit the airlift. Tip the clean gravel on top, sloping it slightly from the back to the front. This will make it easy to spot any gross dirt accumulating here, which can be removed with aquarium cleaner.

3. Set the rockwork and other tank decor securely in place, once it is clean, before starting to pour in water. Place a saucer on the gravel, and tip the water on to this, so that the gravel beneath is not disturbed.

4. Once the aquarium is about a quarter full, you can add any plants. Do not set the crowns below the level of the substrate, as this will cause them to rot.

5. Put in the heaterstat if you have chosen this system of heating, but do not switch it on until the tank is full. Add a power filter if you are going to use one.

6. Top up the tank, adding sufficient dechlorinator/water conditioner plus beneficial bacteria to seed the filter. Check all the electrical equipment is working correctly.
Place the thermometer on the front of the tank and then leave for several days to check everything is functioning correctly, before acquiring the cichlids.

7. Place a background that matches the environment created in the tank itself behind the aquarium. These are available from aquarist stores, being sold in dimensions to suit aquariums of various sizes.

🔼 Here, (top) the gravel is in place together with two concealed air-stones. So-called paddle-stones are being built up to produce a kind of "reverse cascade." Below, the rock decor is positioned and the diffused air outlets are turned on to be checked.

CHAPTER 4

Feeding Habits and Food

*The current popularity of cichlids has bred a range of special diets, whether just for discus (*Symphysodon *species) or for particular categories of cichlids, such as those with essentially vegetarian feeding habits. Just like us, cichlids require a mixture of carbohydrates, fats, and proteins, augmented with vitamins and minerals, in order to stay healthy.*

There is a tendency to group cichlids on the basis of their diets, but this should only be taken as a guide. Studies involving cichlids in the wild have revealed that most are opportunistic feeders, and are likely to prove omnivorous.

Within Lake Victoria, for example, so-called piscivorous species such as members of the genus *Prognathochromis* normally prey on other fish but have been known to eat algae. Similarly, those that are generally perceived as being herbivorous have been recorded as preying regularly on shrimps and other aquatic invertebrates. This is probably a reflection of the availability of food, but other factors, such as the age of the fish, may be significant.

Young cichlids are likely to have a higher requirement for the key amino acids, which serve as the building blocks of protein, than adults. These essential amino acids are not present in plant matter, and so at this stage of life, when they are growing fast, even herbivorous cichlids will tend to become more predatory.

MOUTH FACTORS

Other factors, notably the size of their mouths, constrain their feeding habits. Angelfish (*Pterophyllum* spp.), sometimes sold young for inclusion in a community aquarium, risk having their fins nipped by more agile tank occupants, such as barbs (*Barbus* spp.). If the angelfish survive, they are then likely to prey on much smaller companions once they are large enough to swallow these other fish.

The shape of the cichlid's mouth helps to indicate much about its general lifestyle as well as its feeding preferences. Cichlids, having adapted to live at all levels within the water, vary significantly in this respect. Those that seek food at or near the surface have upturned mouths, possessing a lower longer jaw, as seen in the case of jewel cichlids (*Hemichromis bimaculatus*). Species that feed in midwater areas have evenly balanced jaws while cichlids feeding at or near the substrate have a longer upper jaw. This elongated upper jaw is evident in Fuelleborn's cichlid (*Labeotropheus fuelleborni*), a

◑ The jewel cichlid (*Hemichromis bimaculatus*) is basically an omnivorous species although live foods are favored, and especially useful as a conditioning food to encourage spawning. The "upturned" mouth–actually a long lower jaw–reveals a preference for foods at or near the surface.

herbivorous species from Lake Malawi. But the structure of the jaws reveals only part of the story.

The pharyngeal jaws, found at the back of the mouth, give a clearer insight into the fish's individual feeding habits. These teeth help to move food through the upper digestive tract so that it can be swallowed more easily. The shape of the teeth here, as well as that of the jaws themselves, differs between different groups of cichlids. As might be expected, the teeth are least developed in those cichlids that feed on fine particles such as algal plankton.

Predatory cichlids have a very different pharyngeal dental pattern, with sharp, so-called papilliform teeth, which can tear up their prey. They resemble the teeth in the outer jaws, in effect reinforcing their action. Those cichlids that feed on snails, such as *Cichlasoma aureum* from Central America, are equipped with pharyngeal teeth resembling human molars, allowing them to crush the shells of the snails

⬆ Young oscars. The diet of cichlids may alter as they grow older, partly because adults of some species such as oscars (*Astronotus ocellatus*) grow to a relatively large size. When older, their gut can absorb vegetable nutrients more efficiently.

with relative ease. The pharyngeal muscles themselves are correspondingly well developed for this purpose. However, these muscles will atrophy to a certain extent if these cichlids are fed instead on a substitute diet. So it is heavy use of the musculature associated with the teeth that keeps them toned.

FOOD, DISTRIBUTION, AND DIVERSITY

Feeding behavior has a major impact on the distribution of some cichlids, notably the mbuna, which is the local Chichewa term for the rock-dwelling cichlids occurring in Lake Malawi. The algae growing on the rocks tightly restrict their areas of distribution here. Such is their dependence on these rocks that they will not swim over intervening sandy areas (which may be only a few feet across) to reach new feeding grounds. Populations have therefore become very localized, which helps to explain why there are so many different forms of the same species, evolving in isolation.

The high population densities of these cichlids are in turn made possible by their feeding habits, which help to minimize direct competition for food. Among the herbivorous species, the Malawi golden cichlid (*Pseudotropheus auratus*) has strong teeth that enable it to pull strands of algae off the rock or bite through them. In contrast, the fish known locally as mbuna kumwa (meaning "rock tapper") uses its double row of teeth to rasp at the algae. Its fearsome teeth occupy so much space that it cannot close its mouth fully.

Studies of this unique lake habitat have revealed that there are often in excess of 300,000 invertebrates, ranging from shrimps to midge larvae present in an area of just 10 square feet (1 square meter). Many mbuna have adapted to feed on these creatures too.

◑ Eduard's mbuna (*Pseudotropheus socolofi*) from Lake Malawi is less specialist in its feeding habits than a number of other cichlids occurring in the lake. Specializing in certain types of food has its advantages–less competition–and its disadvantages–sensitivity to environment changes not suffered so acutely by the omnivores.

The Malawi blue cichlid (*Pseudotropheus zebra*) has yet another means of feeding, by sucking the algal strands directly from the rocks. Yet it can also use its teeth like those of a comb, to strip out invertebrates hiding among the algae there.

Other cichlids have progressed from feeding on algae to eating the scales of others of their own kind. Given the relatively high densities of mbuna populations, they are guaranteed a plentiful supply of food. Perhaps not surprisingly, species like the Malawi scale eater (*Genyochromis mento*) are not popular aquarium fish.

Cichlids occurring in Lake Victoria also display significant divergence in their feeding habits. Mature males of the blue nyererei (*Pundamilia azurae*) prefer to feed on plankton in the water, whereas females and young feed on algae. There are also predatory species here too, such as members of the *Harpagochromis* genus, and even more specialized feeders: *Lipochromis*, for example, use their large mouths to grab hold of mouthbrooding cichlids, forcing them to release their developing young.

Central American species

A similar diversity in feeding habits can be seen in Central American cichlids as well. *Neetroplus nematopus,* found in rocky areas of Lake Nicaragua, feeds on algae that it strips off the rocks using its sharp,

⬆ Nyassa blue cichlid (*Pseudotropheus zebra*). This Malawian cichlid will eat a variety of greenstuff, including algae, as well as aquatic invertebrates. The lips are a big clue to its feeding habits.

chisel-like teeth. These are almost identical in appearance to the dentition of *Eretmodus cyanostictus*, a species with a corresponding lifestyle in Lake Tanganyika.

Greatly enlarged lips are another feature seen in species of both New World and African cichlids, surely linked with their diets. The lips can be anchored around a small hole in rockwork where an invertebrate is lurking, in effect creating a seal to allow the prey to be sucked out more easily. The constant trauma of the lips rubbing against the rough surfaces causes them to swell up in size.

The lips of these fish do not normally become so highly developed when such cichlids are kept in aquarium surroundings. This provides further evidence to support the suggestion that their labial enlargement has a mechanical rather than a tactile significance. The rougher the rockwork is in the wild the more pronounced the enlargement. In areas where red devils (*Amphilophus labiatus*) and midas cichlids (*A. citrinellus*) occur together, only the red devils display the fleshy lips described in their scientific name. In localities where midas cichlids occur in isolation, some populations may develop this characteristic too. This suggests that red devils generally have more specialized feeding behavior and could be dominant over midas cichlids.

One of the most frustrating behaviors of some Central American cichlids in particular is their desire to dig in the aquarium substrate. This reflects the way in which such fish will naturally comb the sediment in search of edible items, ranging from algae to crustaceans and snails. The whole shape of the cichlid's head may be modified accordingly, with the eyes being located at a relatively high position on the sides of the head. This in turn enables the fish to burrow more deeply with its lips into the substrate. Again, where the sand is coarse, the lips of these cichlids are also more swollen, as they are better suited to the mechanical effort of digging in such surroundings.

Other substrate feeders can operate more effectively in the shallows, keeping their bodies more horizontal at this stage, and having flatter but nevertheless extendible snouts, as exemplified by the firemouth cichlid (*Thorichthys meeki*). They tend to filter through

The red devil (*Amphilophus labiatus*) is also known as the thick-lipped cichlid. The prominent lips are a particular feature of male fish.

the substrate, rather than digging into it in search of edible items to such an extent.

It seems clear from a study of the cichlids from Central America that a number of today's species, including some that are herbivorous, are actually descended from insectivorous ancestors, which then developed more specialized tastes. They include the fruit-eating *Cichlasoma tuba*. The inherent adaptability of the cichlid's mouthparts has certainly contributed to the current diversity in form and lifestyles.

AQUARIUM DIETS

Although cichlids display such a range of feeding behavior, it is possible to persuade even those that are not tank-bred to take substitute diets. You must nevertheless have a clear idea of the feeding habits of the specific cichlid fish to ensure that you are offering as similar a diet as possible. For those that feed mainly on algae, then a diet containing spirulina is recommended. Those that prey on larger aquatic invertebrates such as shrimps can be given a basic carnivore diet, augmented with other items. In each case, a formulated diet will contain additional vitamins and minerals to meet the needs of the fish. This in turn can be supplemented with other items to add variety to the diet. Even plankton-feeding cichlids can be catered for quite easily in aquarium surroundings, as they can

⬆ The demonfish (*Satanoperca leucosticta*) from northern South America is a peaceful, almost sociable species in spite of its name. It seeks its food on the floor of the aquarium. The position of the eyes high on the sides of the head is a clue to this behavior. Unusually for cichlids from this part of this world the young retreat into their parents' mouths if danger threatens.

often be encouraged to eat flake food as well as a variety of small aquatic live foods.

The way in which food is offered will have an impact on how readily it is taken. Flake foods are thin and float on the surface, making them ideal for those species that usually occupy the upper reaches of the aquarium. Pellets, on the other hand, will normally tend to sink, so they are more suitable for fish that are found in the middle and lower areas of the tank. The size of the particles of food being offered is significant, even in the case of prepared diets. Flake is only suitable as a regular diet for smaller fish, with larger individuals preferring food sticks. These are short lengths of food, which will remain floating for a relatively long period, thanks to their low density.

Although small fish can eat larger pellets, they are not able to swallow them whole. By nibbling chunks off as they soften, fish can obtain nutrients. But the pellet tends to disintegrate in the process. This is significant because as the pellet breaks into small fragments, the debris is likely to accumulate on the floor of the aquarium, ultimately increasing the level of pollution and the burden on the filtration system. This can be especially significant for a recently established tank, where the filter is not fully developed. Be sure to match the size of pellets to what the cichlids can comfortably consume: If in doubt, use smaller rather than larger pellets.

⊙ A range of prepared and fresh foods can be offered to cichlids, including all of these dried foods. Guess what? Large pellets are best fed to large cichlids.
A. Pellets
B. Large pellets
C. Banana
D. Food sticks
E. Flakes

Live foods

Although aquatic live foods feature in the diets of many cichlids, there is a significant risk to using them as fish food, because they can easily introduce diseases to the aquarium. This can be in the form of harmful bacteria and fungi, as well as parasites. There can also be storage problems with such foods, and fish food manufacturers have adopted several strategies to overcome these difficulties.

Gamma-irradiation has been used for preparing aquatic live food for many years. The food is prepared and placed in sachets, before being irradiated to kill any harmful microbes. A wide range of fish foods is available in this form, including *Tubifex* worms, water fleas (*Daphnia*) and bloodworm (*Chironomus*). It is possible to obtain more unusual items in this way, such as shrimp, krill, and plankton. Being fresh rather than dried, these foods need to be kept in a freezer until

⊖ Water fleas (*Daphnia magna*) seen under the microscope. These crustaceans are popular food with smaller cichlids, but should be cultured if possible and then sieved out of the water for the fish. This reduces the risk of introducing disease or parasites to the aquarium.

required, but they are generally available in small packs so that it is easy to take out and defrost what is needed without any wastage, cutting the blocks carefully with a sharp knife.

The latest innovation in this field is individual sachets of sterilized food, which come suspended in a special jelly that is free of preservatives, but supplemented with vitamins. The nozzle attaching to the sachet means that you can regulate the amount of food being offered to the fish. The choice of live foods available in this form is relatively restricted, however, compared with gamma-irradiated foods.

The third option for prepared live foods is freeze-dried food. This, as its name suggests, comes in a dried form and has the advantage that it can be stored without problems at room temperature. It is a useful stand-by, if other foods such as gamma-irradiated foods are not available. A number of the foods available in this form, such as krill, brine shrimp (*Artemia*), and bloodworm, are just as good. River shrimps, which are ideal for larger cichlids, can also be obtained in this form. However, freeze-dried live food is less palatable than other types of food. This should be considered in the case of newly acquired or sick fish whose appetites may not be good.

Fresh live foods

It is still possible to purchase fresh aquatic live foods suitable for cichlids, in spite of the dangers that they can pose to the health of

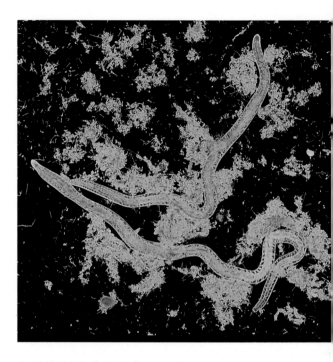

○ Magnified living *Tubifex* worms, in among organic debris. They represent a potentially harmful although popular live food for cichlids. Freeze-dried *Tubifex* is a safer option, but not as palatable.

the fish. *Tubifex* (tubificid) worms, for example, are found in mud in water containing high levels of organic waste, as in the vicinity of sewage outfalls. Similarly, bags of *Daphnia* can contain other aquatic creatures that may kill small fry. This is not to say that fresh live foods cannot feature in the diets of cichlids, and food of this type is undoubtedly beneficial. It can help to maximize the coloration of the fish naturally, and also acts as a good conditioner, stimulating a desire to spawn.

Depending on where you live, as well as the time of year, it should be possible to harvest some live food of your own, which will be relatively safe. Simply leaving a bucket of water out may be sufficient to attract gnats to lay their eggs there. These soon hatch into actively swimming larvae, which can be caught easily using a small strainer and tipped into the aquarium as required. It may also be possible to set up a culture of *Daphnia*, transferring them to a well-established tank where there are plenty of algae growing.

Terrestrial live foods bred commercially for the herptile market can give variety to the diet of larger cichlids. It is not a good idea to offer mealworms (*Tenebrio molitor*), however, because the hard outer casing of chitin around their bodies is relatively indigestible. Although the fish may snap up these invertebrates, they are likely to be regurgitated soon afterward. On the other hand, molting mealworms, which are recognizable by their whitish skin covering, can normally be used quite safely as fish food.

Other options to consider include crickets, which are available in a variety of sizes, but are not especially easy to store. This is important when you consider how few the cichlids will eat each day. A new possibility is curly winged flies, which are a mutant form of the house fly (*Musca domestica*); their wing tips curl forward, making it impossible for them to fly successfully.

One of the traditional foods offered to larger carnivorous cichlids such as oscars (*Astronotus ocellatus*) are earthworms (*Dendrobeana veneata/Lumbricus terrestris*). These can obviously be dug up in the back yard, and left in a box of damp grass for 48 hours or longer, to cleanse their digestive systems of any harmful elements they might have ingested. As a safer alternative, you can buy the smaller sizes from live food suppliers, offering these whole to your fish.

Fresh foods for herbivorous cichlids

It can also be beneficial to supplement the diet of vegetarian cichlids. A first step would be to encourage the growth of algae in the aquarium, but you can also buy a variety of vegetables. Try to buy organic foodstuffs and always wash these off thoroughly in dechlorinated water. Spinach, red lettuce, and fresh or defrosted frozen (but not canned) peas all work, but only in small enough quantities to minimize wastage because it can be difficult to remove the debris. It may help to place the greenstuff in a special clip attached to the side of the aquarium. This allows the fish to feed easily, and you can simply lift out any greenstuff that is left uneaten.

Without enough greenstuff in their diet, predominately vegetarian cichlids are likely to nibble at the aquarium plants. This still applies even if they are given a suitable food, simply because the nutrients in the commercial foods tend to be concentrated, and the fish may not be receiving sufficient fiber in their diets. They then follow their natural instincts to eat plants in their surroundings. It can help to include floating vegetation, especially robust and fast-growing duckweed (*Lemna* spp.).

PREDATORY FEEDING ADAPTATIONS

Specialist piscivore species and those that take other relatively large prey such as river shrimp will aim to capture their quarry so it can be swallowed head first. This in turn ensures that any sharp projections, including scales, will not become caught in the throat. This upper part of the digestive tract extends so that cichlids are able to swallow relatively large prey. The stomachs of predatory species have a highly acid pH to assist with the digestion process, before the food passes lower down into the intestinal tract, where the nutrients can be absorbed into the body.

PISCIVOROUS CICHLIDS

There is an inherent difference between the digestive tracts of herbivorous and piscivorous cichlids. Those that feed primarily on plant matter have a long digestive tract, and depend on having a bulky diet because of its typically low nutritional value. Predatory cichlids have a shorter digestive tract, their food having a higher nutritional value.

Whereas plant matter is important for vegetarian cichlids, there is no need to offer guppies or other small fish as food for piscivorous species. Quite apart from any personal misgivings, there are risks that such fish could introduce unwanted pathogens, including parasites, into the cichlid tank. Given the range of live food that is now available, there is no need to use so-called "feeder fish."

A number of fish keepers do supplement the diet of predatory species with mammalian sources of protein, notably offal in the form of beef heart. This can be harmful, however, because the fish find it difficult to digest its relatively high fat content. It pollutes the tank as well.

Risks of overfeeding

The type of diet that the cichlids require also influences the frequency of feeding. Follow the instructions on the food package but as a guide, the fish will require two or three meals each day. Take care to offer no more food than will be eaten within five minutes of being placed in the tank. Young fish that are growing will require more frequent feeding than adults. Overfeeding is even worse if there are no other fish to eat any leftovers in an aquarium housing cichlids on their own. Bear in mind that in the wild, vegetarian species will be feeding almost constantly, whereas carnivorous species will tend to digest a meal before seeking another.

In cases of overfeeding, predatory cichlids will vomit up partly digested food, thanks to the muscles that link the wall of the esophagus with the throat. This vomited food will rapidly decay hidden in the tank, causing a sudden rise in the ammonia level; the stomach acid vomited up will also add to the deterioration in water quality. If in doubt about how much to feed, be mean,

The peten cichlid (*Petenia splendida*) can grow up to 20in (50cm) long, and so requires large commercial formulations at this stage. Live foods are preferred.

especially with predatory fish. They are at particular risk of growing to an excessive, bloated size. The problem can become acute in the case of the larger Central American cichlids, and it is likely to shorten their lifespan.

Food for young cichlids

Brine shrimp nauplii are a valuable rearing food for young cichlids, and these invertebrates are also recommended for plankton-eating species. Brine shrimp (*Artemia salina*) are purchased in the form of eggs, which need to be kept in an airtight container to exclude moisture; otherwise, not so many will hatch. In the wild, they occur in salt flats, and their number can vary from year to year, depending on the rainfall.

It is now possible to purchase complete hatchery kits, offering the simplest means of producing a ready supply of these tiny crustaceans at home. The special hatching salt simply has to be mixed with dechlorinated water. The eggs are then added and kept aerated with an airline. It helps to obtain shell-less eggs, since the eggshells themselves are indigestible and cannot be fed to the fish.

🠕 Overfeeding of predatory species such as the jaguar or managua cichlid (*Nandopsis managuense*) is likely to shorten their lifespan.

Kept at a temperature of 75°F (24°C), the young brine shrimp larvae should hatch after about 36 hours. They can then be caught and transferred to a separate tank using a special sieve supplied as part of the kit. In this case it is the eggshells that float, while the brine shrimp congregate at the bottom of the container, so separating them is not too difficult. Dip the brine shrimp in dechlorinated freshwater before offering them to the fish.

FEEDING STRATEGIES

The vast majority of cichlids search actively for food during the day, but there are exceptions, notably *Cyphotilapia frontosa*, which is most active in feeding during twilight periods. Plankton feeders move in accordance with their food, which may alter its level in the water, often preferring to feed at the start or end of the day. These cichlids usually feed close to the surface of the water, where they find these schools of microscopic plant matter called phytoplankton and associated creatures, known as zooplankton. Plankton-feeding cichlids are often observed moving in an unusual way at this stage. As the waves at the surface carry the schools of plankton, the fish also bob up and down in the water, feeding on them.

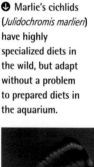

⊕ Marlie's cichlids (*Julidochromis marlieri*) have highly specialized diets in the wild, but adapt without a problem to prepared diets in the aquarium.

Other predatory species may become active after dark, hoping to catch their quarry unawares. Not all such cichlids benefit from feeding under these circumstances, especially those that hunt other fish. Some will simply root about in the substrate, seeking aquatic snails, whereas others prey mainly on shrimp. Perhaps the most remarkable

are those cichlids that manage to feed on freshwater sponges, which can prove to be a positively hazardous meal. A few cichlids, such as *Julidochromis marlieri* from Lake Tanganyika, seek out these invertebrates despite the glasslike spicules that their bodies contain, as well as their protective toxins.

Teamwork

Cichlids may also rely on the company of their own kind to provide them with food. Small species sometimes shadow larger species as they stir up small edible items, including invertebrates, which they can dart in and eat. For larger fish, the movements of their companion can warn of approaching danger, so that there can be benefits to both parties.

There is evidence that some cichlids hunt in schools working alongside each other like dolphins. Cichlids in the Cameroon lake of Barombi, for example, will steal food from other aquatic creatures, particularly crabs. The natural agility of these fish allows them to dart in and seize their quarry out of the crab's claws, displaying behavior known to zoologists as kleptoparasitism, which is best noted among seabirds that rob others of their catches.

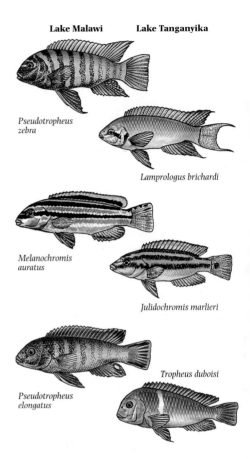

Lake Malawi   **Lake Tanganyika**

Pseudotropheus zebra

Lamprologus brichardi

Melanochromis auratus

Julidochromis marlieri

Pseudotropheus elongatus

Tropheus duboisi

More predatory cichlids have also adapted to meet their individual diets. The scale-eating, or lepidophage, species are a case in point. Their unusual behavior was first confirmed from Lake Malawi in 1947, and has subsequently been recorded elsewhere. Members of this group of cichlids have evolved a variety of feeding strategies, some of which are much more aggressive than others. Some lepidophage cichlids actively ambush their targets, while others adopt a more passive approach. This behavior has led to their developing an appearance that allows them to blend in as a member of a school, so they can approach an intended victim without being detected.

The most highly specialized lepidophages have even developed a jaw structure that deviates to one side of the body, making it easier to rip off scales while swimming alongside another fish. The mouth itself can be slanted either to the right or left. The appearance of these cichlids is genetically determined, and they can only feed on one side of the body.

◑ Some cichlid genera from Lake Malawi and Lake Tanganyika have developed remarkably similar body shapes as they have come to exploit similar niches in the food supply.

CONVERGENT EVOLUTION

There are a number of parallels between the lifestyles and specialized feeding habits of cichlids in both Lake Malawi and Lake Tanganyika (*see diagram, page 89*). These parallels are sometimes described as convergent evolution. The feeding pattern of *Nimbochromis livingstonii* in Lake Malawi, for example, was long thought to be unique in the vertebrate world: It mimics a dead fish, lying on the substrate and attracting and then attacking would-be scavengers. Amazingly, however, another example of this behavior pattern has emerged in the case of *Lamprologus lemairii*, from Lake Tanganyika.

It seems likely that lepidophagy may have evolved from the way in which some fish clean others, removing parasites from their bodies. Just as on coral reefs, where their marine relatives, the wrasses, often serve as cleaner fish, so certain cichlids have evolved to fill this niche in the Rift Valley lakes. *Docimodus evelynae* even feeds on fungus growing on the sides of fish while it is young, before going through a phase of eating invertebrates and plankton. It then moves to deeper waters, actively attacking the scaleless catfish (*Bagrus meridionalis*) and feeding on its flesh, as well as pulling the scales off other cichlids that it encounters.

Cannibalistic hunters

In spite of the dedicated parenting behavior associated with cichlids in general, some species prey on the eggs and fry of other fish, as well as those of their own kind. Egg stealing is a relatively common phenomenon in cichlids, with the predator striking when a spawning pair of mouthbrooders is at its most vulnerable. This is the stage immediately after egg laying and before the female has been able to collect up the eggs into her mouth. Although the spawning male will attempt to drive off the interloper,

◗ In spite of the efforts of the parent fish to protect their brood, like this red devil (*Amphilophus labiatum*), some–the majority in fact–will fall victim to predators, possibly other species of cichlid, or fish of the same species. Sometimes the parents themselves will devour their own fry.

Dow's cichlid (*Amphilophus dovii*) is a predatory species, but its young may themselves be hunted by other cichlids, notably the midas cichlid (*Amphilophus citrinellus*).

the egg thief succeeds in about half of all attempts. Compared to other cichlids, which produce hundreds or even thousands of eggs, mouthbrooding cichlids lay only tens of eggs. Losing several of these to an egg thief is consequently very serious.

Nor is it always effective for fry to seek the safety of their mother's mouth. Some hunting species, such as *Champsochromis spilorhynchus* from Lake Malawi, harass a mouthbrooding female to call her brood back to her. They then swoop in to feed on the offspring as they attempt to get back into her mouth. Other species batter a mouthbrooding female about the face, forcing her to release her offspring and sometimes killing her as a consequence.

Recent research findings suggest that this type of interspecific predation on eggs is not confined to Old World species. Underwater observations carried out in Lake Xiloa, Nicaragua, reveal that some midas cichlids (*Amphilophus citrinellus*) display similar behavior. Individuals occupy an area of territory above the breeding site chosen by the larger and piscivorous Dow's cichlid (*Amphilophus dovii*), which can grow to 20in (50cm) in length. In common with many New World species, *A. dovii* breed and lay their eggs on the substrate. The young are then corralled into a spawning pit until they are free-swimming. Researchers found that a midas cichlid would repeatedly swoop down, taking both eggs and subsequently the fry, which hatched about 48 hours later. This strategy was risky, however, and not just because *A. dovii* is itself a piscivore. The greater size of these cichlids, combined with their strong parenting instincts, suggests that they will attack in defense of their nest site. The dead midas cichlids observed near some nests had almost certainly been killed by *A. dovii* as a consequence.

CHAPTER 5

Gender and Communication

Some owners are convinced that, rather like dogs, their cichlids can come to recognize them. Remarkably, there is evidence to support this view. There can be an element of so-called conditioning involved, however. When the same person feeds the fish at roughly the same times each day, a routine can develop.

Yet it is no coincidence that it is the larger cichlids such as the oscar (*Astronotus ocellatus*) that seem to form the strongest bond with their owners, just as they naturally do with a mate. They would have no difficulty in distinguishing one face from another looking at them through the aquarium glass, just as they can distinguish their mates by visual means.

SEX CHANGES

The subject of cichlid recognition opens a fascinating area of study, with many interesting findings. In the case of some monogamous cichlids, the loss of a mate can result in a remarkable change. The females of some species actually alter gender during their lifetime—a characteristic known to biologists as protogyny—following the loss of a mate. In the case of most vertebrates, the individual's gender is predetermined by means of a pair of sex chromosomes. Yet the situation is much more complicated in cichlids. Studies reveal how in the first place, the water chemistry can affect the gender of the young fish.

So-called temperature sex determination (TSD) can be significant because, like certain freshwater turtles, some species of cichlid apparently possess no sex chromosomes to predetermine their gender. The impact of TSD has been studied most closely in the South American dwarf cichlids, which form the genus *Apistogramma*. When their eggs are kept in water at higher temperatures, male fish are likely to be produced, with the key determining period apparently being not so much during hatching, but rather when the young are between 30 and 40 days old. Similar results have been recorded with the young of some mouthbrooding African species, such as the Nile mouthbrooder (*Oreochromis niloticus*).

These observations have triggered investigations into whether the pH of the water could also have an effect. It was discovered that more female *Apistogramma* cichlids were bred as the pH rose. The situation is not clear-cut, however, and varies from cichlid to cichlid. The offspring of kribensis (*Pelvicachromis pulcher*), a West

African species, can also be modified by the pH of the water in which the eggs are being kept. In other cases, such as the dwarf Egyptian mouthbrooder (*Pseudocrenilabrus multicolor*), neither pH nor water temperature had any impact on the gender of the young cichlids. This is an area that requires further study in the wild, particularly in the case of the *Apistogramma* genus itself, where a single male will mate with a number of females, forming no individual pair bond. Natural selection would mean that an imbalance in the gender of hatchlings in favor of females should therefore be beneficial to the species as a whole.

Adult transformation

The most interesting observation perhaps, based on aquarium cichlids, is how some species are still capable of modifying their gender even once they are adult, depending on their surroundings. Such behavior is apparently widespread with the group, as it has been recorded in cichlids originating from the Americas, Africa, and Asia. The change has been well documented for example in the case of the orange chromide (*Etroplus maculatus*), which is a monogamous species. When two females, housed under laboratory conditions, spawned as a pair on their own, scientists assumed that the eggs would be infertile.

⬆ Borelli's dwarf cichlid (*Apistogramma borellii*). Water temperature can influence the gender of the fry of members of this genus. The eggs, laid on a cave roof, take four to five days to hatch. The male takes a more active part in protecting the fry than some other *Apistogramma* species.

Remarkably, a small percentage of the eggs hatched. This confirmed the premise that if denied access to a male for mating purposes, then hormonal changes within the female's body could lead to an individual developing functioning testicular tissue. The trigger could actually prove to be stress, in the case of this monogamous species. The stress caused by being deprived of a natural partner may increase the output of cortisol. This hormone is closely allied to the sex hormones in terms of its chemical formulation. Acting on the sex organs, cortisol could bring about the partial change in gender.

AGGRESSIVE BEHAVIOR

It is likely that it will be the more aggressive of the two fish that switches gender, based on research involving midas cichlids (*Amphilophus citrinellus*). Scientists had previously believed that the structure of the brain cannot be altered significantly during life, but again, this has been disproved by studies involving the reproductive biology of cichlids. The hormonal output from the hypothalamus to the pituitary glands leads to the release of hormones that act specifically on the testes, causing them to enlarge. The testes themselves then release another group of hormones known as androgens into the bloodstream, triggering aggressive behavior. This influx causes male fish to become more aggressive and territorial as they become ready to spawn. But the neurons—

⬇ A pair of tiger cichlids (*Nandopsis festae*) mouth-wrestling. This test of strength is often used to resolve apparent disputes without more serious conflict.

⊖ A two-spot pike cichlid (*Crenicichla lepidota*) with its mouth open strikes an aggressive pose. The fins are extended–and this doesn't look like a bluff! But fighting is a waste of energy and a risk, even for the victorious fish, so ritualized chest beating precedes actual combat. This is a predatory species, originating from parts of Brazil and Bolivia.

the nerve pathways—in the brain, responsible for triggering this release also grow in size at this stage, before regressing later.

Even aggressive cichlids will try to avoid the physical stress and exertion inherent in fighting, partly because there can be no certainty about the outcome. Caught unawares in combat, both fish could even fall victim to a passing predator. Each therefore goes through a series of stylized rituals, in the hope of persuading their opponent to back down. They seek to increase their size, adopting a more frightening posture by raising their gill covers so they stand out from the sides of the head. Their body coloration is intensified too. As a last resort, the fish spread their fins and open their mouths just prior to conflict, as they swim at each other, still leaving a window of opportunity to escape at the last moment.

Physical encounters

Jaw wrestling as a test of strength is very common behavior in many cichlids, and can lead to the formation of a pair bond in the case of young fish. One cichlid will finally pull its head away to one side, dragging the weaker individual with it. This can be the end of the dispute, or it may escalate into further combat, sometimes described as carouseling. During this phase of fighting, when serious harm can be inflicted, each fish attempts to bite at the body or fins of its opponent. Once one grabs a hold, it will anchor itself in place, which may in turn allow the other to retaliate in a similar way. In the resulting spin, each tries to break free. This process calls for a considerable amount of physical effort: The combatants may both stop for a period, and engage in a further bout of mouth wrestling.

Ultimately, it finally reaches the stage where the weaker individual seeks to escape, but although this is possible in the wild, the space within the aquarium means that it may not be feasible. The stronger cichlid then pushes home its advantage, which is likely to lead to the death of its opponent. This is why it is so important not to stock the aquarium in such a way as to allow fighting among these highly territorial fish. You also need to keep a close watch on the cichlids for any signs of imminent serious combat, removing the weaker individual before it can suffer any serious harm. Fight injuries can lead on to life-threatening infections in some cases, not to mention permanent disfigurements even if the fish recovers.

Aquarium responses

The way in which the aquarium is stocked can have a direct influence of the likelihood of fighting in these surroundings. Some Rift Valley cichlid keepers stock aquariums for mbuna to the maximum safe level. They reason that by keeping more fish together, even aggressive contacts between individuals are correspondingly brief. This strategy, however, can lead to a deterioration in water quality. It is vital to remember partial water changes and to ensure the filtration system is highly efficient. It may also place the cichlids under greater stress, although they can sometimes be found living at high densities in the wild. Another finding, which throws interesting light on the causes of aggression in these fish, is that outbreaks of aggression are significantly fewer when males are housed on their own, with no females present in the aquarium.

Catching

Sometimes even if you have done everything right—the correct tank size, decor, and inhabitants—aggression will still occur. In which case, a quarantine tank (see page 118) comes into its own again. Do not hesitate to remove a fish under attack, because serious injury or death are distinct possiblities. (The following advice is relevant to transfer a fish for any reason, not just to save one under attack.)

A catching net is essential in transferring cichlids from one aquarium to another. Such nets are available in various sizes, although it can be difficult to find a net long enough to catch angelfish (*Pterophyllum spp.*) successfully, because of their body height. It may be easier under these circumstances to use a plastic bag, allowing it to fill with water

and then steering the fish into the bag. It should enter the bag easily, thanks to its narrow body shape. You can use the same method with discus (*Symphysodon* species), which have a similar profile.

When using a net, try to avoid disturbing the aquarium decor. You could otherwise end up dislodging rockwork with dire consequences. Always switch the power supply off and disconnect it first, before servicing the tank in any way, to protect yourself from any electrical injury that could easily be fatal. Rely on stealth as far as possible to net the fish, approaching it from beneath, or encouraging it to swim over the net.

Having caught the cichlid, transfer it back to water as soon as possible, but keep your spare hand over the top of the net until then, so there will be no risk of the fish jumping out and ending up on the floor. Most nets have fine mesh to allow you to transfer young cichlids without difficulty. Still, you should always check that none is accidentally left behind in the net when you have finished transferring them to their new accommodation.

🔾 Jack Dempsey cichlids (*Nandopsis octofasciatus*) are both territorial and aggressive fish by nature. A "balance of power" has to be established in the aquarium between them, even if they are a pair.

Reproduction

CHAPTER 6

One of the most fascinating aspects of cichlids is the parental care that most species lavish on their eggs as well as their offspring. This behavior is unexpected in fish, but you can witness it first-hand because many cichlid species reproduce readily in aquarium surroundings. A failure to spawn is often the result of inadequacies in the aquarium environment, rather than problems with the fish themselves.

➊ White-spotted cichlids (*Tropheus moorii*). These fish are still too young to breed. Adults, which are variable in appearance, show totally different patterning. Adult males may harry females. Starting with young fish and being patient can help to avoid this problem.

It must be said, though, that breeding cichlids has its share of trauma, usually linked to the aggressive nature of these fish. Take great care over introducing potential partners. Although some cichlids can form strong pair bonds, they can also be highly aggressive toward each other. The risk is highest in the case of two male fish, but the threat can be just as great with members of the opposite sex introduced under unsuitable surroundings. Others need to be kept in groups, typically comprising one male and several females, in order to promote harmony in the aquarium.

PLANNING AHEAD

With compatibility proving to be such an important hurdle, it can help to acquire immature young fish at the outset and grow these on together, allowing them to form natural bonds as they would in

the wild. It is then a matter of transferring compatible pairs to separate tanks as they grow older if you have a monogamous species. You will be able to spot signs of compatibility by observing the fish closely. Look for fish that swim closely together, sometimes nudging perhaps at each other's flanks. It should be possible to identify the pair when you need to move them by careful observation of their markings. Always transfer them to a new setup at the same time, so that there is no risk that one of these territorial fish will take over the tank and attempt to drive off its former companion.

This process can be an expensive means of setting up pairs, especially in the case of larger cichlids. It is best begun in a specialist fish house or room where there is space for a couple of tanks, rather than in a domestic setting. Prepare for this upheaval, and the inevitable costs in growing on the young fish, by planning in advance. A successful spawning by angelfish (*Pterophyllum* spp.) for example can produce several hundred fry, and they will need more space as they grow.

Inquire early on to see whether local aquatic stores may be interested in taking some of the young fish. Alternatively, concentrate on mouthbrooders because they generally produce smaller broods of offspring. Mouthbrooding imposes physical limitations on the number of eggs that can be accommodated in the mouth, but it also means that more of the fry should survive through the critical early stages of life.

THE QUICK ROUTE

A possible shortcut to breeding monogamous cichlids successfully is to invest in a proven breeding pair, but this can be costly. It will also take some time for the fish to settle down in their new environment before they express any interest in starting to spawn. The loss of one member of an established pair can also raise difficulties in terms of pairing the surviving cichlid up again in due course. Fighting remains a huge risk.

Never try to add a single individual to the existing aquarium, even after a suitable period of isolation, because the established fish will almost certainly harass it relentlessly. This behavior will soon prove fatal. The best hope of ensuring compatibility is to transfer both cichlids to a new setup, where neither has a territorial advantage. It may also help to lower the water temperature slightly and to feed a fairly simple diet based on prepared foods rather than live food, to lessen any inclination to spawn. Another option, depending on the size of the aquarium, may be to separate the fish by inserting a divider in the tank. You can remove this after several weeks and allow the pair to swim together. Move any decor around so that in

effect the aquarium becomes a new environment. You will need to watch the cichlids carefully in either case in order to minimize any risk of fighting.

Water conditions

Cichlids from stable environments such as the African Rift Valley lakes will spawn in similarly stable water conditions in the aquarium. However, those originating in river systems such as the Amazon may benefit from changes in water chemistry. Such species often spawn after heavy rainfall, which "freshens" the water by altering its composition and making it softer.

You can best replicate this in the aquarium by means of a fairly dramatic water change, removing far more than would normally be taken out routinely. As a guideline, some breeders lower water levels to a point that just allows the cichlids to continue swimming. The fresh dechlorinated and conditioned water can then be allowed to flow slowly into the tank through a siphon tube, which will be less disruptive both for the fish and the aquarium in general than pouring it directly from a bucket.

Adding more live food to the diet can help to stimulate spawning. This also reflects what occurs in the wild. Invertebrates multiply rapidly when the surrounding land becomes flooded, providing the fish with a glut of high-protein food. In the aquarium, you can use whiteworm, although this live food needs to be cultured from a starter pack, as it is not normally available in commercial quantities.

Such cultures need to be set up well in advance of the anticipated spawning, since it will take a month or more for them to start becoming productive. Partially fill a small tub with a peat substitute,

and then make shallow holes with a pencil. Put a batch of starter-pack whiteworm in these holes, on top of some bread soaked in a little milk. Cover and keep the culture relatively warm, replenishing the food as necessary. When the worms are ready to harvest, they can be separated easily from the medium by tipping them into a shallow saucer of water taken from the aquarium. Most cichlids will eat these worms greedily.

⬆ A rainbow over the Amazon River. Seasonal increases in rainfall alter river flows and can serve to stimulate breeding behavior in cichlids. Water changes can be used to similar effect in the aquarium.

FOOD FOR THE YOUNG

It is vital to provide suitable rearing food for the young cichlids. Obtain a brine shrimp hatching kit and a sufficient supply of eggs. As a guide, start the first culture when you carry out the major water change, since this should ensure that there are brine shrimp nauplii available in the critical early stages. Cultures will need to be set up in sequence, to ensure an adequate supply for the young cichlids once they are free-swimming; the adult fish can eat any surplus.

Ensure that the decor within the aquarium is suitable for encouraging the fish to spawn successfully. The individual requirements of these fish differ significantly. A study of their spawning behavior reveals that the most primitive cichlids, occurring in Madagascar and Asia, lay their eggs on the substrate, as do the majority of those occurring in the New World; but those found in the Rift Valley lakes display much greater diversity in their reproductive behaviors, with mouthbrooding being commonplace.

There are also significant differences in cichlid mating patterns. The simplest arrangement is monogamy, as in angelfish (*Pterophyllum* spp.), where male and female form a pair bond. In some cichlids, this may last just until egg laying, but often, it continues through until the young are independent. In other mating systems, males may not be involved at all in looking after their offspring. Males will typically fertilize the eggs of more than one female under these circumstances, although this can still happen with a structured community. The harem system, for example, is common among the smallest cichlids, such as members of the *Apistogramma* genus. The territory of the colorful and much larger male is split into smaller areas occupied by a number of breeding females.

Another variation is called lekking. Males congregate in distinct display areas and are visited by females when they are ready to spawn. Each male constructs actual display sites, using sand in the shallows. The competition faced by lekking males to mate in the wild is fierce, although females are likely to have their eggs fertilized by more than one male. This means that the offspring in a brood can have different paternal genes. There can be as many as 50,000 males coming

⊕ ⊖ Behavior patterns change in the period before spawning takes place. This female Ramirez's dwarf cichlid (*Microgeophagus ramirezi*) is seeking a spawning site with her larger male partner.

together along just a 2.5-mile (4.2-km) stretch of Lake Malawi shoreline, competing for the attentions of females of their species.

Mouthbrooders are most numerous in Africa. It typically takes about three weeks for the young to emerge for the first time, although the range can be from 12 to 35 days, depending on the genus. Although the task of guarding the eggs is usually the responsibility of the female, who will not feed during this period, there are some exceptions. The most notable example is the blackchin mouthbrooder (*Sarotherodon melanotheron*), where the male is entirely responsible for looking after the eggs. This is also one of the few monogamous mouthbrooding species.

Some other mouthbrooding cichlids, from both Lake Tanganyika and Lake Victoria, stay together after mating. Once the female releases the offspring from her mouth, they can dart back to relative safety in the mouths of either member of the pair. Nor is it always just the parents who look after the fry. In some cases, members of a previous brood may subsequently remain in the breeding territory, helping to watch over younger siblings before they themselves start breeding.

PAIRING

One of the most difficult aspects of successful tank breeding is finding a compatible pair. In the case of midas cichlids (*Amphilophus citrinellus*), males ultimately grow to a larger size than females, but there is always a considerable overlap in size between the sexes. These monogamous cichlids form a lasting pair bond, with the male invariably linking with a smaller female regardless of his own size.

It is difficult to sex such fish externally on the basis of anything other than their tiny genital papillae, located on the underside of the body. On close examination, these structures tend to be more disk-shaped in females; the male's papillae have a longer, more pointed shape. It becomes easier as the time for mating draws close. Males often develop a distinctive swelling, called a hump, on their foreheads. The male's throat also swells, but not to such a significant extent.

Interestingly, male cichlids with this characteristic develop larger humps in aquarium surroundings than those in the wild. It might be thought that males with more prominent humps were most attractive to females. Instead, it is those whose humps correspond to the appearance of wild midas cichlids that seem to evoke the strongest pairing response. This suggests that the hump itself is not a sign of strength so much as a visual clue to the cichlid's sex, which a female can easily identify from some distance away. The development of the male's hump is quite rapid. Instead of being the result of changes in fat stores, it is caused by a build-up of fluid called edema, which dilates the tissues.

RECOGNIZING A MATE

There is still much to be learned about the phenomenon of mate attraction in cichlids. Visual recognition does appear to be a vital element in the case of many species, as was proved by a classic series of experiments involving the West African jewel cichlid (*Hemichromis bimaculatus*). The researchers investigated the role of color in mate

⊕ The appearance of cichlids often changes as they mature. A number of male Central American species like the midas cichlid (*Amphilophus citrinellus*) portrayed here develop a pronounced swelling on the head called the nuchal hump as they mature. The midas cichlid on the right is a non-breeding male. The swelling usually develops at the time of pair formation.

recognition, devised special blindfolds for the fish and also anesthetized them to slow their movement. They concluded that the cichlids could distinguish the gender of other individuals that they encountered by differences in their swimming patterns.

The role of odors, as a means of sending out sexual signals, may be significant in some cases. Most likely, special chemicals called pheromones are released into the water as females come into spawning condition. Even more fascinating, however, is the possibility that vocalizations could be significant in pairings. Male *Cichlasoma centrarchus* have been found to utter series of low-pitched grunts, calling more frequently when they encounter a female. Significantly, once courtship behavior is underway, then the frequency of these calls (which are only audible to us when amplified) decreases, suggesting there is a link between the vocalization pattern and pairings. The same laboratory research proved that it is possible to influence the behavior of males by playing back aggressive calls of other fish, confirming that these calls can elicit a behavioral response. The sounds in question are not made using vocal chords, but by grinding the pharyngeal teeth.

Visual clues can be important for females seeking a mate of their own species, particularly in areas such as Lake Malawi, where there are a number of different nest sites constructed by various cichlids. Each species has evolved its own distinctive style of nest. This may consist of towering heaps of sand. Females swimming over the area can identify with a nest built by a male of their own species.

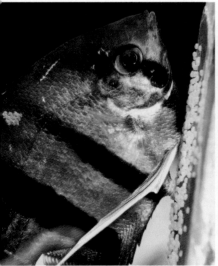

◑ Angelfish (*Pterophyllum scalare*) laying eggs on a pre-cleaned spawning site (left). The male (right) removes the fry to a new leaf "nursery" two or three days after hatching.

The egg spots present on the anal fins of male haplochromis cichlids clearly have a vital role to play in the reproduction of these species. They resemble eggs in appearance, and are there for a good reason in the case of these mouthbrooding species. The female fish will seek to draw these spots into her mouth, believing them to be eggs. This in turn causes the male to release his milt, allowing fertilization of the eggs already present in the female's mouth to take place. Research has shown that those males with the greatest number of such spots trigger the most spawnings.

Although it is tempting to suggest that body markings play a key part in mate recognition in monogamous cichlids such as angelfish (*Pterophyllum* spp.), this is not necessarily the case. The unpatterned golden morphs of the midas cichlid (*Amphilophus citrinellus*), for example, appear to be able to recognize their mates just as readily as fish that display distinct markings.

It does seem, however, that it is the side view that is significant, probably combined with the individual swimming motion of the fish. Facial characteristics must be important in this respect, and this is where markings can help to distinguish individuals. At close quarters, odor recognition may also play a part, as has been shown experimentally by the convict cichlid (*Archocentrus nigrofasciatus*). Females kept in the dark, confronted with both their own partners and strange fish, proved to be far more aggressive toward the interlopers.

SPAWNING BONDS

For breeding purposes, cichlids can be divided into two groups. The substrate spawners will utilize a wide variety of sites, rather than just laying their eggs in a pit excavated in the substrate as their name may suggest. Some are reasonably adaptable in terms of their spawning preferences, utilizing rockwork or plants in their aquarium. Others, such as *Apistogramma* dwarf cichlids, which are sometimes described as cave-spawners, require a suitable retreat under which they can lay their eggs. In the aquarium, this retreat may take the form of an overhang of slate or a submerged clay pot. Smaller cichlids, which would be more vulnerable to predation, tend to be cavespawners, with larger, more aggressive species seeking to breed in the open.

There is often but not always a strong pair bond between these substrate-spawning cichlids. It is less commonplace among the second group, the mouthbrooders, with males taking the opportunity to mate at random with any females that are ready to spawn. This follows through in the differences between parental responsibilities. Whereas the task of guarding the eggs and caring for the fry is split in the case of the monogamous species, the female mouthbrooder usually carries out these tasks on her own.

These considerations affect the way the cichlids are kept for breeding purposes. The sex ratios are significant for mbuna cichlids from Lake Malawi, one of the most widely kept groups of mouth-brooders. Housing such fish in individual pairs will result in the female being harried, while keeping several males with females is likely to lead to fighting. As a result, these cichlids should be accommodated in groups of one male with perhaps four females.

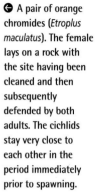

⊖ A pair of orange chromides (*Etroplus maculatus*). The female lays on a rock with the site having been cleaned and then subsequently defended by both adults. The cichlids stay very close to each other in the period immediately prior to spawning.

● While is it
impossible to describe
all the ideal setups
for the very many
cichlid breeding
methods, one clear
division is between
open spawners, like
discus, angelfish, and
chromides for
example, and cave
spawners, like most of
the dwarf cichlid
species.

THE ROLE OF THE AQUARIUM

Designing the aquarium to accommodate the spawning preferences of the adult fish greatly enhances the likelihood of breeding success. It should also reduce outbreaks of aggression arising from the inability of the pair to find a suitable spawning site. Studies of convict cichlids (*Archocentrus nigrofasciatus*) have revealed that these cave-spawners prefer the darkest enclosure, and that it should only have one entrance. You can create such a setup with a clay pot, allowing the adult cichlids to guard their eggs effectively. Most cave spawners are believed to use the roof of the cave for spawning because there will be less risk of the eggs becoming partially buried by any accumulation of silt on the floor.

The advantage of spawning in the open is that with a good flow of water the eggs will be kept well oxygenated, although they will need to be stuck in place to resist the current. The Asiatic chromides face a particular difficulty in finding adequate spawning sites in their native brackish sandy lagoons. The green chromide (*Etroplus suratensis*) digs down to create a pit exposing the roots of sea grass, attaching its eggs here, which blend in alongside the root nodules so they are almost impossible to distinguish. Similar behavior has been observed in Central American species, where there are few if any opportunities for anchoring eggs in place on a sandy base. The Nicaragua cichlid (*Cichlasoma nicaraguense*) performs a remarkable feat in constructing a nest for the eggs in the clay banks of rivers. Starting with a small hole, the male fish will insert his dorsal fin into this opening, and turn it round repeatedly in order to drill out a nesting chamber.

Playing on parental instincts

One of the underlying reasons for cichlid success is that they typically have strong parental instincts. Even substrate spawners will anchor their eggs together to prevent their drifting off on the currents, as occurs with many other groups of fish. Studying the eggs laid by the more primitive cichlids, such as the chromides (*Etroplus* spp.), can provide some insight into how this process began. Sticky filaments providing anchorage are located at one end of the egg, opposite to where the sperm entered to fertilize it. Most other substrate spawners have shorter adhesive threads over the entire surface of the egg, which would appear to give better scope for attachment. The eggs are laid neatly and close to each other. How the female achieves this is unclear, as she cannot see them at this stage, although it is thought that the pelvic fins probably assist in this process.

Mating itself can sometimes be hit-and-miss, particularly in cases such as the snail-dwelling lamprologine cichlids from Lake Tanganyika (*see* page 132). There is simply not enough space for the

Open spawners

Cryptocoryne spp. Numerous species of this hardy plant are available, tough enough to withstand the attentions even of some of the larger cichlids.

Hygrophila spp. Water wisteria can provide a hiding place for fry.

Anubias spp. Prefers low to medium lighting, as do the angelfish that may be prepared to lay their eggs on its leaves.

Hairgrass (*Eleocharis* spp.) can be used by species that like to hide their fry in the vegetation after hatching.

Ornate wood preferred for spawning by some species

Java fern (*Microsorum pteropus*). Tolerant of a wide range of temperature and light.

Corkscrew vallis (*Vallisneria torta*). Can help to provide depth of vegetation suitable for, say, discus.

Rocks, including a flat, horizontal surface suitable as a spawning site for many Central and South American cichlids. For many species, it should be in a position that can be defended.

Substrate of the correct coarseness or fineness for those cichlids that dig a pit to spawn or to hide their fry, like kribensis. Too coarse and the female cannot excavate successfully.

Cave spawners

If this is purely a breeding tank, then plants are not strictly necessary.

Plenty of rocks creating cavities and ledges; be sure they are all securely positioned.

Shell for *Lamprologus* species of Lake Tanganyika, and others. Provide a selection, as some individuals are quite choosy.

Fine substrate.

Clay pots are ideal for those species that require a spawning site with only one entrance, and those that naturally attach eggs to the "roof" of the cave.

Undergravel filter is not really the best option as much of the floor area is covered with rocks. A power filter is better.

male to enter this spawning chamber. As a result, he is forced to release sperm close to the entrance, in the hope that they will be able to swim across and fertilize the eggs. *Apistogramma* dwarf cichlids also use this method, which developed from spawning patterns in small caves of their native South America.

Males do run the risk of being cuckolded, notably in the case of at least one of the snail-spawning cichlids from Lake Malawi, *Lamprologus callipterus*. Rival males of this species can manage to mate undetected with members of the dominant male's harem, thanks to their significantly smaller size. This allows these interlopers either to dart down at the moment of mating, ejaculating their sperm into the shell, or, perhaps even more deviously, to enter the shell itself and mate with the female there. The resemblance of these smaller males to mature females allows them to move unhindered by the established male.

⊕ A female
Lamprologus callipterus
inspects a potential
spawning shell, which
will be big enough for
her to enter but too
small for the male
partner. It may not be
too small however, for
other, opportunistic
suitors. (See text.)

There are actually more documented species that engage in this so-called parasitic spawning to be found within the cichlid family than any other group of freshwater fish. It is probably no coincidence that the largest number in total are to be found in the case of wrasses, which are marine relatives of cichlids. Such behavior is possibly even more common in aquariums than in the wild, especially when high stocking density in a tank creates greater opportunities.

On occasions, it may appear that the cichlids' parental instincts have deserted them. A most extreme example occurs when pairs of discus (*Symphysodon* spp.), spawning for the first time, consume their eggs. This behavior can occur among mouthbrooders too, being triggered by a catastrophic fall-off in the number of eggs or fry. It then makes more sense for a female to mate again, in the hope of rearing more fry, in what is a short lifespan, rather than devote her energies to just a few offspring. As a result, the female may actually eat her offspring.

EARLY DAYS OF LIFE

Once they have laid their eggs, substrate spawners will remain close to them. However, in some instances, as with the green terror (*Aequidens rivulatus*) and related species, it is the female who assumes greatest responsibility for looking after the eggs, while the male seeks to protect the pair's territorial boundaries. The adult fish fan the eggs with their fins, maintaining a flow of water and thus oxygen over their brood. When the eggs start to hatch (with the

time interval being directly influenced by water temperature), the parents assist their offspring in breaking through the eggshells.

At this stage, just a few days after laying occurred, the young cichlids are still in a highly undeveloped state. They are known as wrigglers because that is all they can do. Some cichlids, especially cave-spawners, have a pit in the substrate where they can shepherd and guard their helpless offspring at this stage. In other cases, wrigglers may be carried in their parents' mouths and physically stuck on to leaves of aquatic plants.

Studies of rainbow cichlids (*Herotilapia multispinosa*) have revealed that water conditions have a marked effect on this pattern of behavior. In their natural habitat, where oxygen levels in the water are quite low, the adult fish will transfer their young to plants near the surface, where there is more dissolved oxygen in the water. With the higher oxygen levels of an aquarium, however, rainbow cichlids will choose a pit in the substrate, while reverting to their natural behavior if the oxygen in the aquarium is deliberately lowered.

Keeping the young all in one locality obviously carries its risks, and to avoid possible predators, some cichlids move their broods regularly to new pits. The movement of the young cichlids brings the benefit that their combined tail movements serve to create a local current of water that carries away waste and brings oxygen to the group.

Getting going

Within a week the young have digested the remains of their yolk sacs and are likely to have started swimming. However, they need to be closely chaperoned by the adult fish at this stage, to ensure

⬆ Trewavas' cichlid (*Labeotropheus trewavasae*)—a mouth-brooding species from Lake Malawi—seen here with young.

that they stay in the school. Adult fish spot any that swim off, retrieving them in their mouths and spitting them back into the group. In most cases, the fry then drop down to the substrate. Notably, this does not occur in the case of angelfish (*Pterophyllum* spp.), which are found in densely vegetated stretches of water, as this response could lead the young cichlid to lose sight of its group. An adult fish swimming off slowly could lead to confusion, drawing some of the fry with it and splitting the family group. In order to avoid this possibility, the adult fish takes off very abruptly, giving the brood no opportunity to accompany it.

In spite of the dedicated care of both parents, cichlid broods are decimated by attacks from predators. Few of the young fish will ultimately survive, but they are safer in schools than they would be swimming on their own through the critical early days of life. As the brood grows older, the adult fish will embark on excursions with them, often well outside their home territory. They remain in touch, and either parent can send out a danger signal, known as jolting, by rippling their body. The pelvic fins are distinctively colored to reinforce this signal in various species. This movement creates not only an unmistakable visual danger alarm but also creates a local current in the water.

Young cichlids tend to be predatory in their feeding habits at first, which is why tiny creatures such as brine shrimp (see page 87) are needed for rearing purposes. This applies even in species that turn out to be herbivorous as they grow older, and is not just because of their protein requirement to sustain growth. There is no space in the young cichlid's body for a lengthy digestive tract, as found in adult members of herbivorous species.

⬇ As soon as they are free-swimming, young discus (*Symphysodon aequifasciatus*) obtain nourishment from mucus produced on the flanks of their parents.

Contacting and concealing

Pairs of substrate spawners may produce food on their flanks for their fry. The fry swim up to the sides of adult fish and nibble the mucus there—a process called contacting. This in turn stimulates the mucous cells in the skin to swell up and increase their level of secretion. In the early stages after the fry become free-swimming, there is more than nutrition to be gained in this way. Two hormones are present here—growth hormone and thyroxine, which is usually produced from the thyroid glands and has a key role to play in the body's metabolic processes. Both have been

shown to aid the development of the young fish.

A different approach is required for substrate spawners when the female is responsible for rearing her offspring alone, as with the dwarf *Apistogramma* cichlids of the New World. They inhabit waters where there is plenty of natural cover, so it is not difficult for the female to find suitable retreats in which to conceal her fry. The offspring are well camouflaged so they can blend in well against the dark background, and are naturally reluctant to move. They lurk close to the substrate instead of swimming in the body of the water. This behavior should dictate the aquarium's decor. Similar patterns of behavior exist among those Lake Tanganyika cichlids where the female is responsible for the care of the brood.

Joining the ranks

Sometimes it seems that the number of fry has increased after they have become free-swimming. There are several possible explanations. The fry might become confused and join up with another family; others may actually be stolen. Some of the fry might even belong to a different species of cichlid, but provided that they are not larger than the young cichlids in the existing group, they will be accepted. (Larger individuals are likely to be eaten.) This arrangement may actually benefit the host parents. Studies reveal that those fry that transfer to a new brood are less likely to survive, certainly in the case of convict cichlids (*Archocentrus nigrofasciatus*), giving the original fry a better chance.

⬆ The male and female discus (*Symphysodon aequifasciatus*) are separated in the tank by a wire mesh to prevent the male from harassing his mate (left). The female discus watches over her 2-day-old fry (right) fanning and guarding them. The eggs were laid on an earthenware cone now protected by meash to prevent them being eaten.

The many-spotted or cuckoo synodontis (*Synodontis multipunctatus*), native to Lake Tanganyika, actually uses mouthbrooding cichlids to hatch and care for its own young. The female catfish lays small batches of eggs, which are swept up by a spawning mouthbrooder. These then develop alongside her own eggs, although they are significantly smaller in size. The young catfish utilize their yolk sacs within just three days—well before the cichlids would have completed their development. As a result, they start to feed on the cichlid eggs, growing very fast and wiping out the brood.

Once released from the female's mouth, these young catfish will still dart back here at first if danger threatens, and she is totally oblivious to the fact they are not her offspring. This behavior is probably quite widespread in the wild, since a study in the lake discovered cuckoo synodontis in the mouths of six different cichlid species, including *Tropheus moorii*. So if your aim is to breed these cichlids, remember to steer clear of these catfish!

HYBRIDIZATION

Inadvertent hybridization can crop up in a breeding setup for Rift Valley cichlids. It is especially likely in the case of haplochromis species because they will mate together readily in an aquarium, where there are none of the barriers that separate the fish in the wild. The likelihood of such unplanned matings is even greater if the tank is home to a range of unpaired fish, so that it may be safer to concentrate on a particular species. Hybrid cichlids are potentially very damaging to the development of captive strains of these fish if they themselves are fertile, diluting the characteristics of the individual species. Many of these species—particular African cichlids—have relatively small distributions in the wild. And with threats such as pollution increasing, there is a growing need to build up captive strains.

One of the most controversial breeding programs of recent times has given rise to the so-called parrot cichlid. No one is sure of its precise origins, although the original breeding program may have been undertaken in Asia. For some time, its ancestry was unclear. It is now known that these fish are the result of hybridization between the midas cichlid (*Amphilophus citrinellus*) and the firehead cichlid (*Vieja synspilum*). Their color can vary

from shades of yellow through to blood red and recently purple, with those individuals displaying the more intensive red shades being preferred. It is unclear what the future may hold regarding creating new forms of artificial cichlid developed for traits such as color. But the recent development of the first genetically modified aquarium fish suggests this is set to become a highly contentious area.

MUTATIONS

Sometimes a change in the genetic material alters the appearance of the affected fry. These changes are often harmful to the species, particularly in the wild, where these young cichlids are most vulnerable to predators. More elaborate fins can slow their swimming, while a change in color means they are likely to be more conspicuous to a passing predator. Within aquarium surroundings, however, unusually colored individuals are just as likely to survive as their normally colored companions. The breeding of such mutations is still controversial among some fish keepers, but it has become commonplace for various cichlids, such as angelfish (*Pterophyllum* spp.), where a wide range of color varieties is established.

Odd color varieties are associated with a number of other species, such as the golden variant of the ram (*Microgeophagus ramirezi*). Once a mutation of this type has arisen, it may then be possible to improve the depth of color by selectively breeding from the best examples, evolving what is then often described as a strain.

⬅ The so-called red parrot cichlid is not a naturally occurring species but a hybrid created by crossbreeding. This type of breeding program is highly controversial, although these particular fish–including the purple variety shown here–are now quite widely available.

Establishing aquarium strains

Inevitably, there will be changes in aquarium strains as the result of domestication, affecting behavior as well as appearance. There is a tendency to aim for the most colorful examples, which breeders hope will thrive in the absence of predators. But over time, the maternal instincts of the cichlids may start to wane, even in the case of mouthbrooding species. One of the most effective ways of overcoming this particular problem is to incorporate what are sometimes called "dither fish" in the aquarium alongside the cichlids. These fish should have robust, lively natures and although they will not actually molest the cichlids, their presence elicits protective behavioral responses. One of the best choices for Rift Valley species are the colorful rainbowfish belonging to the family Melanotaeniidae, although these are not native African fish.

To establish breeding species successfully in aquarium surroundings you must ensure that you pair unrelated fish together. Try to be sure that your initial breeding stock is unrelated, and keep a careful log of matings, so that you can avoid pairing closely related cichlids. Otherwise, over a period of time, there may be problems such as a reduction in the number of eggs being laid or an increase in the number of deformed fry. Lack of vigor, size, and loss of color may be other characteristics that emerge under these circumstances.

BREEDING DIFFICULTIES

Aggression on the part of the male fish can hamper your attempts to spawn cichlids successfully. You can watch for signs of trouble before the female is seriously weakened, but then deciding on the best solution is a problem. Reintroducing them after a period of separation can be difficult. It is therefore a good idea to invest in a divider; this creates a barrier in the tank, but at the same time will allow the cichlids to mate.

A popular choice for this purpose is a plastic light-diffusing panel from a hardware store. The panel prevents the fish from having direct contact, but it is still possible for fertilization to take place through this divide. The other advantage is that it should be easier to reintroduce the cichlids later, as they will have remained in contact with each other throughout the spawning period. The level of aggression tends to decline after this period.

On occasions, some mouthbrooding cichlids will reject their eggs prematurely, but it is possible to hatch these independently, preferably in a clear container with small holes to allow for a flow of water through the unit. This can be constructed very easily using the base portion of a plastic mineral water bottle, with gentle aeration here. Once the fry start to appear free-swimming, they should be allowed out into the surrounding environment of the aquarium where they are to be reared. This can be equipped with a simple sponge filtration system, which represents no danger to the young fish. If a mouthbrooding cichlid dies while caring for her brood, it is possible to rescue the young and rear them in this fashion. They will require fry food such as brine shrimp nauplii once they have absorbed the yolk sacs on the underside of the body.

Removing the young

Provided that the aquarium is relatively large, it is possible to leave the young there for some time. Watch for any signs of aggression from the parents that suggests that the young should be removed without delay. It is very important to have a setup already established, however, so as to minimize the stress on the young fish when they are moved. The water there should have been adequately matured, using water taken from the original tank.

⊕ Egyptian mouthbrooder (*Pseudocrenilabrus multicolor*). If disaster strikes during the incubation period eggs can be hatched and fry reared artificially.

CHAPTER 7 # Lifespan and Diseases

Living in the relative security of the home aquarium means that most cichlids survive much longer than those in the wild. As a guide, most of the smaller Rift Valley species have a natural life expectancy of about 18 months in the wild, but can live for double this period in a tank. Larger New World species may have a lifespan of a decade in such surroundings.

⏷ A quarantine tank must supply the bare necessities. While it is difficult to prove that adding plastic plants helps the healing process it seems logical that it might benefit a stressed or injured fish.

There can be drawbacks given such a life of apparent comfort, not least the fact that with ready access to food, these fish can become obese. An abnormal variance in size between males and females may also arise, thanks to differences in their metabolism. Female mouthbrooders regularly undergo periods when they do not eat anything for weeks at a time, and they have to invest considerable body resources in their relatively large eggs. This means they are at a potential disadvantage compared with males, who will grow faster and ultimately reach a larger size. Should this discrepancy become too large, then females are vulnerable to being persecuted by their mates.

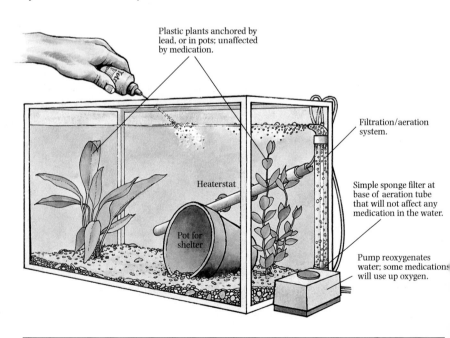

Plastic plants anchored by lead, or in pots; unaffected by medication.

Filtration/aeration system.

Heaterstat

Pot for shelter

Simple sponge filter at base of aeration tube that will not affect any medication in the water.

Pump reoxygenates water; some medications will use up oxygen.

COPING WITH A CRISIS

It helps to have a spare tank and heating system available, along with a basic sponge filter. This can be used as a treatment tank for sick cichlids, with an infection less likely to spread if a diseased fish is removed from the main aquarium at the earliest opportunity. The spare can also accommodate an individual that has been attacked. Cichlids can be surprisingly savage when launching into an attack on their own kind: The stress of constant harassment can prove fatal to the weakened individual unless the pair is separated without delay. In a clean tank, it will be easier to treat injuries such as torn fins successfully and allow the injured individual to recover.

Some of the health preparations on the market contain natural compounds such as aloe vera, which assist the healing process. Proprietary medications—also available from aquatic stores—can be useful for treating common cichlid ailments such as fungus and white spot. Remember that some of these are based on dyes such as methylene blue, which can stain the aquarium sealant. That is another good reason to keep a separate tank for treatment purposes.

Passing through a filter containing carbon will deactivate most chemical treatments. Remember also that they may depress the beneficial bacteria established as part of a biological filter. This in turn can lead to an unexpected falloff in water quality, leaving all the fish in the main aquarium at greater risk of becoming ill if the treatment is introduced here. When using any medication, be sure to follow the instructions for diluting the chemical carefully. Underdosing may not be effective, and an overdose could prove fatal for the fish.

⬇ A firemouth cichlid (*Thorichthys meeki*) suffering from body fungus. An infection of this type can often start with a minor injury to the body, which then allows the fungus to take a hold.

Stress impact

Illness is most likely to strike in the case of newly acquired fish, or when the environmental conditions are less than ideal, because this imposes stress. In a mixed collection of cichlids, however, not all are equally susceptible to deterioration in water quality. A sudden loss of

particular species in a tank of Lake Tanganyika cichlids, for example, often indicates that the pH is becoming acidic. This emphasizes the need to carry out regular monitoring of water conditions, even if everything appears to be running smoothly.

With a tank, there are inevitably microbes that could cause infection in weakened fish. These opportunists are often various types of fungi, which can gain access quite easily to the body through any injury to the scales. If the cichlid's immune system is impaired, then the infection will soon become apparent. The symptoms of most fungal infections resemble absorbent cotton, covering the affected part of the body and spreading rapidly if untreated. In the wild, cichlids seem to have evolved a unique way of dealing with fungal infections. A number of species will eat such growths, particularly when young, presumably giving the affected fish an opportunity to recover.

● Dwarf cichlids are highly sensitive to diseases often linked with poor water quality. This *Apistogramma nanpesi* is suffering from white spot.

Feeding on fungus is not that far removed from consuming the mucus that parent fish produce as food for free-swimming fry. It is widely seen among Rift Valley species and among members of the Asiatic genus *Etroplus*. Green chromides (*E. suratensis*) attract the attention of their smaller orange species (*E. maculatus*) by adopting a pose resembling that used by adult fish when encouraging their offspring to feed. They position themselves upright in the water, with their body quivering to attract attention. Another unusual attribute of such behavior is the way in which the color of the green chromide darkens, which helps to highlight the whitish fungal stands.

Young fish seem to be at greatest risk of developing infections, as their immune system may not be functioning as effectively as that of adults. It is suspected that there could be an immunoglobulin-like substance in the mucus that they eat, which affords them some initial protection from

● Another dwarf cichlid, *Apistogramma gibbiceps*, with hole-in-the-head disease; difficult to spot in such a small fish.

infection. In the case of discus (*Symphysodon* spp.), this early link between adults and offspring is even more vital. Special cells are transferred across as part of the feeding process and the young discus also obtain beneficial bacteria, which in effect "seed" their intestinal tracts. These microbes presumably help to facilitate the digestive process while providing a barrier to potentially harmful pathogenic bacteria.

Once disease takes hold

Fungal and bacterial diseases can occur together, rapidly spelling the end for a sick cichlid. Poor water quality will result in fin damage, allowing such pathogens to gain a hold. In relatively minor cases, simply improving the fish's environmental conditions can allow healing to take place.

If the infection gains access to the fish's body, then other symptoms such as dropsy can develop. This affects the cichlid's ability to swim effectively as a result of the build-up of fluid in the abdomen, which characterizes this infection. There is usually no effective treatment once signs of dropsy are apparent, but a noninfectious form of this illness is also recognized. Distinguishing the precise cause of fish illnesses is difficult, especially in the absence of laboratory tests, but either your veterinarian or local aquatic store should be able to offer advice. In the (very rare) case of the sudden death of all the cichlids in an aquarium, the cause is more likely to be poisoning of some type, rather than an illness. Try to avoid using any aerosols in particular near the aquarium, since a number of these products contain constituents that can be deadly to fish.

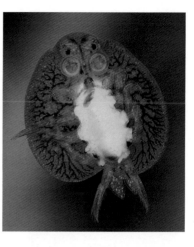

◐ Fish lice (*Argulus* species) are usually found along the fin bases. They are up to ⅓in (1cm) long and almost transparent. They cause the fish to act in a nervous jumpy fashion and to vigorously scratch itself, leading to loss of scales.

Parasites

Some parasitic illnesses encountered in cichlids are universal, meaning that a much wider range of fish can be affected, and stock should be checked very carefully for any signs at the time of purchase. White spot, caused by *Ichthyophthirius multifilis*, is a particularly widespread hazard, partly because these tiny parasites only spend part of their life cycle on the cichlid. The characteristic spots associated with this illness are irritating, causing an affected cichlid to rub its body against objects in its aquarium. These soon rupture, releasing thousands of tiny free-swimming tomites into the aquarium, where they will spread very easily to other fish or reinfect the original host. Each spot can give rise to as many as 1,000 tomites and the debilitating effects of this cycle of infection can in turn lead to secondary infections. If the gills are affected, death can follow quite rapidly.

Treatment entails the use of specific medication to counter the free-swimming stage in the lifecycle, while raising the water temperature slightly will improve the cichlid's likelihood of overcoming the infection. A partial water change can also be advisable, lessening the number of potentially infective tomites that can attack the cichlids. The tomites must find a host within a day or so, because otherwise they will die.

So-called "hole-in-the-head" disease is an illness much more closely linked with cichlids and especially discus (*Symphysodon* spp.). The main cause is the microscopic *Hexamita* parasite, although poor water quality and possibly an inadequate diet may also be implicated. This illness is now often described as "head and lateral line disease," since it invades both the sensory pores on the head, causing loss of tissue here, as well as the lateral line. Cases can be treated successfully with metronidazole, but any associated scarring will be permanent. Given the complex causes underlying this infection, it is probably not a good idea to acquire cichlids that show past evidence of this infection.

Additional risk factors

Environmental factors are also important in the development of other cichlid infections. The actual decor can be a problem in some cases, and for this reason, rough, jagged edged pieces of rockwork should not be left accessible to the fish. Otherwise, they can end up injuring their bodies or even their eyes. This can be a particular problem with some of the large-eyed cichlids from Lake Victoria. A minor scratch in suboptimal water conditions can soon become infected. A special ophthalmic medication will need to be applied to the damaged eye two or three times each day, with the cichlid having to be caught for this purpose so the treatment can be applied out of the water.

An unsuitable diet is believed to underlie cases of what is often described as Malawi Bloat (although cichlids from other lakes in the region can also succumb to this ailment). It is seen primarily in herbivorous species, and particularly if they have been offered high protein diets. This type of food is believed to cause inflammation of the intestinal tract in these cichlids, leading to a loss of appetite and swelling of the body, although the illness may also be linked with the rapid multiplication of harmful protozoa in the digestive tract. These may usually be present here in small numbers but cause little harm under normal conditions. The fact that treatment with metronidazole has been used successfully tends to suggest that a parasitic involvement of this type is significant.

Viral infections

Relatively little is known about viral infections in cichlids, but it is clear that they cause high mortality, especially in commercial breeding setups. At present, there is no effective treatment for such diseases. Viruses tend to attack particular types of fish, with widespread

⬆ As for so many fish diseases, environmental problems—essentially poor water quality in the aquarium—may make discus (*Symphosodon* spp.) susceptible to hole-in-the-head disease.

mortality affecting angelfish (*Pterophyllum* species) having been recorded on fish farms in the Far East. There may be few if any prior signs of illness. Lethargy followed by death for example is characteristic of convict cichlids (*Archocentrus nigrofasciatus*) affected by the Rio Grande perch rhabdovirus, while loss of coordination and appetite leading to emaciation and then death are the recorded symptoms in the case of Ramirez dwarf cichlid virus, which affects *Microgeophagus ramirezi*.

It can help to know the origins of your fish when seeking help for any health worries. Bear in mind that those from the wild are more likely to be suffering from parasites than their tank-reared counterparts. A darkening of their coloration coupled with loose droppings is a fairly typical indicator of the presence of *Capillaria* worms in the digestive tract in discus (*Symphysodon* spp.). Wild-caught Malawi cichlids are prone to being infested with *Acanthocephalus* worms, which cause weight loss. The best treatment in either case is to transfer the cichlids to a separate aquarium where they can be dosed with levamisol, at a typical dose of 2mg/liter, dissolved in the water.

HUMAN HEALTH CONCERNS

The most serious bacterial infection is fish tuberculosis, which typically causes loss of color, spinal curvature and wasting in affected fish, ultimately proving to be fatal. It is a zoonosis, meaning that it is a disease that can be spread from fish to people, although its effects in this case are far less serious than true human tuberculosis. Piscine TB does cause an unpleasant skin infection called a granuloma, which requires antibiotic treatment, the bacteria usually having entered the skin through a cut. Prevention is very simple—wear clean rubber gloves servicing the tank.

You should also never be tempted to suck water through a siphon to start the flow when carrying out a partial water change. There are likely to be unpleasant microbes present here if you swallow any of the tankwater. Instead, fill the tube with dechlorinated water and place your fingers over both ends. Release your finger from the end in the tank first, before lifting your finger from the lower end to create a flow into the bucket. This water should not be tipped down a sink for the same reason, but can be disposed of directly down a drain or in the yard.

○ Stress can affect the coloration of fish, as in the case of this young discus (*Symphysodon aequifasciatus*). The problem may not seem apparent to the inexperienced eye, but this fish—for whatever reason—is almost certainly beyond saving.

CHAPTER 8

Popular Cichlids

NEW WORLD SPECIES

 ### ANGELFISH

Pterophyllum scalare

Distribution: Through most of the Amazon Basin, including tributaries, from Peru right down to Belem at the mouth of the Amazon

Size: Up to about 6in (15cm)

Form: Unmistakably thin body with elongated fins that emphasize its triangular shape. Dark vertical black bands provide disruptive camouflage, breaking up the outline of these fish. There are other, closely related angelfish which can be confused with this

species, such as the deep-finned angel (*P. altum*), which grows larger, up to 10in (25cm) and has bigger fins, as well as the so-called sheepshead angelfish (currently recognized as *P. dumerilii* although probably the same species as *P. scalare*). The relationship between these different forms is unclear at present.

These fish vary in their patterning and coloration through their wide range, but have been extensively bred in aquariums for almost a century. This factor has also contributed to the development of the increasing number of distinctive patterned and color forms, thanks to the inadvertent mixing of fish from different localities. These include marbled angelfish, displaying variable patterning resembling the graining in marble on their flanks, while angelfish with spotted markings are described as leopards. Both forms can also be bred in a golden head or a more vivid redheaded form.

There are also plain gold angelfish too, plus black and silvery-blue variants, as well as so-called ghost angels, which have semitransparent bodies. It is not just the coloration or patterning of these fish that has altered through selective breeding, however. Different fin forms include veiltails (with their more elaborate tail fins), broadfins (where the dorsal fin is

wider than normal), and hifins (which have a much longer dorsal fin). In some cases, the scales are more conspicuous too.

Diet: Will eat a variety of prepared foods, as well as greenstuff, and live foods, which are valuable for conditioning purposes.

Natural habitat and behavior: Often found in heavily weeded stretches of water, where their narrow, elongated body shape allows these fish to weave through the vegetation easily. The barred patterning apparent on their bodies helps to break up their outline in such surroundings. There is no obvious way of distinguishing between the sexes in the case of young angelfish.

A pair will form a strong, lasting pair bond after an initial period of display and some mouth wrestling, although incompatibility can occasionally be a problem. Females swell with eggs in the area behind the pelvic fins and may produce as many as 1,000 at a spawning. These are watched over by the adults, hatching about three days later. The fry are shepherded into a depression in the substrate, and when free-swimming, about eight days after hatching, they are nourished by a secretion produced on the flanks of their parents.

Aquarium conditions: Requires a relatively tall aquarium, typically 15in (37.5cm) or more in height, a water temperature of 75–82°F (24–28°C) and soft, acidic water, with a pH of about 6.5. Often recommended when young for a community aquarium, but likely to outgrow these surroundings rapidly. Long fins are also vulnerable to fin nipping by fish such as tiger barbs (*Barbus tetrazona*) at this stage, which can lead to bacterial and/or fungal infections.

Pairs should be kept on their own for breeding. They will clean and spawn usually on a vertical surface, typically either a piece of slate or possibly on the leaves of an Amazon swordplant (*Echinodorus* spp.). If a pair persist in eating their eggs, you can hatch and rear the fry on their own, by transferring the object on which they have been laid to a separate aquarium. Make sure the eggs are kept well aerated with a fine, gentle stream of bubbles. Adding a fungicide to the water is also sometimes advised. The young can be reared on a suitable fry food and brine shrimp nauplii.

DISCUS

Symphysodon aequifasciatus

Distribution: From the Rio Putumayo in Peru eastward throughout the entire Amazon River basin of Brazil

Size: 8in (20cm)

Form: Very distinctive, discus-like shape, hence their common name. Now ranking as one of the most popular of all cichlids, these fish have been bred in a tremendous range of varieties, which are far more colorful than those seen in wild discus. There are several basic color variants recognized in wild stock. So-called brown discus originated from the lower Amazon region, while a number of fish displaying redder coloration were first obtained from the vicinity of the Amazonian town of Alenquer. The green variety of discus is found in the upper Amazon region, while the so-called royal blue discus come from the vicinity of the Rio Purus and Rio Manacapura, occurring in both the rivers and associated lakes. Such is the distribution of the discus that other localized varieties could still await discovery, particularly in waters occurring west of the Rio Tefe, which have not been well studied.

Working from these basic color variants, a huge number of different varieties have been developed, both by hobbyists and commercial breeders, especially in Southeast Asia. Among the most striking and popular today are the strangely named pigeon blood and the tangerine, which lack spots. The whitish pearl-like spots on their bodies can

identify pearl discus while snakeskins have a decidedly finer patterning. Much plainer are those that are whitish in color, known as ghosts. The actual taxonomy of the discus has long been a matter for debate, with Heckel's discus (*Symphysodon discus*) from the Rio Negro also being involved in the development of today's domesticated forms. (Pictured below is the red spotted leopard discus.)

Diet: Special discus food recommended. Will take freeze-dried live foods too.

Natural habitat and behavior: Found in so-called blackwater areas, discus do not occur in fast-flowing water. Visual sexing is very difficult, especially outside the spawning period, although the members of a pair form a strong bond. They typically lay around 200 eggs at a single spawning, with hatching occurring about two days later. Although young pairs of discus sometimes eat their eggs soon after laying, it is quite normal for the adult fish to assist the young out of their eggs and transfer them on to aquatic plants until their yolk sacs are absorbed and they are free-swimming (usually by five days old). The fry then swim in the company of their parents, feeding on the special mucus produced on the sides of the bodies of the adult fish, which is known as discus milk. Young discus actually have a distinctive elongated outline at this stage, only starting to assume their characteristic shape by three months of age. In a further three months, they will resemble miniature adults.

Aquarium conditions: Discus thrive in a large, relatively tall aquarium, well planted around the sides so the fish can weave in an out of the vegetation. Discus once had a reputation for being rather delicate fish, but they are not difficult to keep, providing that close attention is paid to the water conditions in their aquarium. This water must be soft and acidic, with a typical pH value between 5.8 and 6.6. Adding a blackwater extract to the water, or aquarium peat in the filter (with tannin released from submerged bogwood) will also help to re-create the conditions that these fish are used to, in the wild. The water temperature should be maintained in the range of 75–85°F (24–29°C), with the higher end of this range recommended for stimulating spawning. Water should be changed every three weeks or so. Discus are relatively social fish by nature but become territorial when spawning, when they should be accommodated on their own. This takes place on vertical surfaces, ranging from broad-leafed plants to pieces of slate firmly buried in the substrate. If a suitable site is not available, the female discus may deposit her eggs on the aquarium glass. A heater guard is recommended to prevent them being laid on the heaterstat.

⭐ RAM (BUTTERFLY CICHLID)

Microgeophagus
(Papiliochromis)
ramirezi

Distribution: Rio Meta, Colombia, and through the middle and lower reaches of the Rio Orinoco in Venezuela

Size: Up to 2.75in (7cm)

Form: Colorful with yellowish areas on the front portion of the body, and blue behind, offset with darker markings. Sexing is straightforward, since males have longer, brighter dorsal fins. Some captive-bred strains are more colorful than others; a larger form, sometimes described as the jumbo, has become available over the past decade. There is also a golden form, which has originated through captive breeding in Asia.

Diet: Omnivorous. Can be fed prepared cichlid diets and live foods.

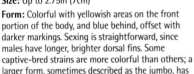

Natural habitat and behavior: Often encountered in savanna pools, which have been created to provide water for agriculture. The water temperature of these surroundings is relatively hot, and the water chemistry is acidic, typically pH5.5–6.3 and soft. Spawning can occur in the sandy substrate, or on a rock. Prior to breeding, the female's belly becomes a more intense shade of red. She may lay up to 200 eggs, which are also red in color, with hatching then occurring about four days later. Males are territorial.

Aquarium conditions: A well-planted tank, with a piece of slate provided for spawning purposes, although a depression in the substrate may be favored. In the aquarium, some pairs prove to retain stronger parental instincts than others. The young cichlids will be free-swimming within a week. Fine fry food is essential at this stage, because they have relatively small mouths and cannot take brine shrimp. Rams often prove to be prolific spawners, with mature females producing eggs every four to six weeks. Their lifespan is relatively short, however, and unlikely to exceed three years.

⭐ JACK DEMPSEY

Cichlasoma
octofasciatum

Distribution: Central America, occurring in the Yucatan province of Mexico, Guatemala, Honduras, and Belize

Size: 8in (20cm)

Form: Dark background color, with traces of black banding and prominent blue markings, not just on the body but extending to the fins. Some strains are more brightly colored, with reddish edging to the dorsal fin. Males are larger and more colorful, with more pointed tips to their dorsal and anal fins.

Diet: Omnivorous, thriving on a commercial cichlid diet plus live foods.

Natural habitat and behavior: The pugnacious nature of these fish is reflect in their name, which commemorates the famous US boxer. Before spawning, the pair will clean the rockwork where the eggs are to be laid. Typically, up to 500 eggs or more may then be laid here, being watched over largely by the female, while the male seeks to drive off any intruders into this territory. Hatching occurs about

three days later, the fry then being herded to pits in the substrate previously dug by the adult fish.

Aquarium conditions: Their care is straightforward, but in view of their highly territorial nature, pairs should be kept on their own. Soft, neutral water heated to 77–82°F (25–28°C) suits them well. When pairing these fish, place them in a new or rearranged tank at the same time, so neither has a territorial dominance. They like to dig, potentially uprooting plants that are not set in small pots. These fish need suitable open areas for swimming as well as retreats, which will (ideally) be used for spawning purposes. The young cichlids can be left with their parents up until the stage when their dark stripes start to become visible, being transferred to separate accommodation at this stage.

RED DEVIL

Amphilophus (Cichlasoma) labiatum

Distribution: Nicaraguan lakes including Nicaragua itself, Xiloa and Managua

Size: 10–13.75in (25–35cm)

Form: Closely related to the midas cichlid (*A. citrinellus*), this species also occurs in a number of different color morphs in the wild, ranging from white through orange to red, with individuals of this latter color being particularly striking. It is those populations occurring in deeper water that naturally tend to be the most brightly colored. While only some populations of its relative develop thick lips, this is a characteristic feature associated with all red devils, as reflected in their scientific name. The lips probably help them to browse more effectively on vegetation growing on rocky surfaces. Males grow to a larger size than females.

Diet: Omnivorous, easy to cater for using prepared diets and live foods.

Natural habitat and behavior: These large cichlids are aggressive, particularly when breeding. Females lay as many as 700 eggs, amber-yellow, on a piece of slate. Hatching typically takes around three days, with the fry being watched over closely by their parents until they are free-swimming, by about a week after hatching. The young cichlids will feed on mucus produced on the flanks of the adult fish.

Aquarium conditions: Pairs should be housed on their own. They need a relatively large tank typically around 4ft (120cm) in length, to accommodate their size, and are likely to dig in the substrate, so that any plants here should be set in pots. A water temperature of 75–81°F (24–26°C) is suitable, and they are reasonably adaptable in terms of water chemistry, thriving at a neutral pH.

MIDAS CICHLID

Amphilophus (Cichlasoma) citrinellus

Distribution: Atlantic waters in Honduras, Nicaragua, and Costa Rica

Size: Typically up to 13.75in (35cm)

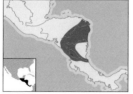

Form: These cichlids range in color naturally from dull gray with black barring through to shades of golden-yellow and orange. These more colorful morphs have been further developed by selective breeding, and are most widely available. Interestingly, in Lago Tiscapa, where there are no other cichlids, selection pressure has not resulted in the development of an orange morph. In Lake Nicaragua itself, however, these cichlids are forced to spawn at greater depths, so bright reddish coloration is beneficial when it comes to finding mates; fry too can locate their parents more easily. In some areas, the lips are enlarged as well. Mature males in all cases can be recognized by the presence of a large nuchal hump.

Diet: Cichlid foods and live foods.

Natural habitat and behavior: Inhabit rocky areas and, unusually among cichlids, even occur in brackish coastal lagoons in western Costa Rica. Live food appears important as a breeding conditioner. A strong pair bond is formed, with breeding occurring in the rainy period, so partial water changes help encourage spawning. Females lay up to 1,000 eggs, which hatch after three days, the fry becoming free-swimming five days later.

Aquarium conditions: Water temperature 70–77°F (21–25°C). Fairly adaptable in terms of water chemistry. These large cichlids often dig in the substrate, so choose and site rockwork so it will not topple over easily. Eggs usually laid in vertical spaces between rocks, so the aquarium layout must be planned accordingly. Retreats in terms of bogwood are also recommended.

⭐ FIREMOUTH

Thorichthys
(*Herichthys*) *meeki*

Distribution: The Yucatan peninsula of Mexico, Belize, and Guatemala

Size: 6in (15cm)

Form: Relatively dark body color, with blue markings on the flanks and fins. Underside of the body, particularly in the vicinity of the mouth and gills is bright red, becoming more intense when the fish are in breeding condition. Their brighter coloration and the more pointed shape of their dorsal and anal fins can identify males.

Diet: Regular cichlid foods for carnivorous species, plus live food.

Natural habitat and behavior: An adaptable bottom-feeding cichlid, which is even found in brackish waters in coastal areas of Belize. One of the most remarkable features of these fish is the way in which their upper lip especially can be extended forward, creating a snoutlike appearance to help them feed in the substrate. There they seek invertebrates such as worms, as well as vegetable matter.

Firemouths produce up to 500 eggs at a single spawning, with the young then being corralled into pits in the substrate after they hatch.

Aquarium conditions: Relatively unfussy about water conditions: pH 7 and medium-hard water will be satisfactory, with the water temperature maintained about 75°F (24°C). This species was one of the first cichlids to be spawned regularly, with breeding records extending back nearly a century in Florida. Pairs do become very aggressive at this stage, and should be housed on their own. A fine substrate is required, which the fish will excavate. Around the sides, some hardy plants can be included, with rockwork being important for spawning purposes. Firemouths may breed several times in the course of a year.

⭐ OSCAR (VELVET CICHLID; PEACOCK EYE)

Astronotus ocellatus

Distribution: The Amazon, Orinoco and Rio Paraguay basins of South America

Size: Up to 13.5in (35cm)

Form: Broad, somewhat rectangular body shape usually with a distinctive orange border to a black spot near the caudal peduncle, at the base of the tail fin, resembling one of the markings on a peacock's tail. Body coloration in the case of wild oscars tends to be grayish, but there is considerable variance between individuals. Some have more widespread orange coloration—a trend favored by captive breeding. Oscars with silvery, orange and blackish markings are described as marbled, while red pearls show very intense reddish-orange coloration over the flanks, broken by black streaks. The so-

called albino variant is not pure white, retaining variable orange markings on the sides of its body. There is a long-finned form. Visible sexing outside the spawning period is impossible, but females then develop raised areas called papillae around their genital opening.

Diet: Prepared cichlid food plus live foods such as earthworms.

Natural habitat and behavior: During pairing, oscars will often appear to battle with each other, but ultimately, they establish a strong pair bond. They attain sexual maturity at about 4.5in (11.5cm) in length. Females can lay up to 3,000 eggs, guarded by both adults, who will shepherd the fry to a pit in the substrate when they hatch about three days later. The eggs are often opaque at first, before becoming transparent.

Aquarium conditions: These fish are capable of becoming very tame, even feeding from the hand. Sand rather than gravel is often considered the best substrate. Water must be low in nitrogenous waste, although chemistry otherwise not too critical. Temperature range 68–77°F (20–25°C).

SEVERUM (BANDED CICHLID; EYESPOT CICHLID)

Heros severus

Distribution: Northern South America to the Amazon basin, but not present in the Rio Magdalena

Size: Up to 12in (30cm)

Form: The presence of a well-defined vertical black stripe on each side of the body near the tail is why these fish are also known as banded cichlids. Young individuals display similar stripes running down the body, but these are not as conspicuous, fading with age. Males can usually be recognized by their more pointed fins and reddish-brown spots and markings on the head. Females develop genital papillae prior to spawning. A more ornamental golden form has also been developed.

Diet: Carnivorous diet with live foods, especially earthworms.

Natural habitat and behavior: These cichlids can be quite selective about their choice of partner, so if possible, start out with a proven pair, or at least look for signs of compatibility before purchasing them. They are unlikely to disturb the substrate and are reasonably compatible outside the spawning period. The breeding behavior of these cichlids is interesting, because although they lay as many as 100 eggs at a single spawning, choosing a flat rock or piece of slate for this purpose, they have occasionally been recorded as mouthbrooding, a behavior more commonly associated with African species.

Aquarium conditions: One of the earliest cichlids to be kept in Europe, introduced to Germany in 1909. Requires water at 75–85°F (24–29°C), with a pH of around 6.5–7. A large aquarium is needed for a pair, with slate or rockwork provided to create retreats and encourage spawning behavior. Plants can also be included, and although they are far less likely to be dug up by these particular cichlids, it is still better to set them in small pots.

GREEN TERROR

Aequidens rivulatus

Distribution: Western Ecuador and central parts of Peru

Size: Up to 10.5cm (27cm)

Form: Two quite distinctive forms exist, with the gold saum (or seam) displaying yellow or reddish edging to tips of its dorsal and caudal fins. It originates from Ecuador, while its silver counterpart, which comes from the Peruvian part of the range, has whitish or silvery coloration here. The body coloration consists of dark spots on a pale greenish background. Females develop darker body coloration as they mature, with less contrast in their markings, while males grow larger and often develop a distinctive hump on their foreheads.

Diet: Requires a carnivorous diet of suitable size, plus live food.

Natural habitat and behavior: Pairs are not social, especially when they come into breeding condition. Up to 300 eggs are laid at a single spawning, on rockwork that the pair has cleaned beforehand. The adult cichlids guard the site, with hatching occurring within four days. The fry are slow to develop initially, and it will take a week until they are free-swimming.

Aquarium conditions: Water at 68–77°F (20–24°C) will be suitable, increased slightly to encourage spawning. Water chemistry can vary from slightly acid and soft to neutral pH and medium hard; it is more important to carry out regular changes of about a quarter of the aquarium's volume, to maintain water quality and prevent a build-up of nitrogenous waste. Their large size again means that the decor in their tank needs to be firmly sited, and plants should be suitably robust. They need to have suitable space for swimming, coupled with retreats created by bogwood, with a careful planting scheme required so as not to block off this open area.

CONVICT CICHLID (ZEBRA CICHLID)

Archocentrus (Heros) nigrofasciatus

Distribution: Central America, from Guatemala to Panama

Size: 6in (15cm)

Form: The distinctive gray background color and black stripes of these cichlids is suggestive of prison uniform, and explains their unusual name. Female convict cichlids are more colorful, with orange suffusion on the sides of their bodies and dorsal fins. Males grow slightly larger, and sometimes develop a hump on their heads once they are mature. Their gray coloration becomes paler when they are approaching spawning condition. This is not a sign of poor health.

Diet: Omnivorous. A suitable cichlid diet with additional greenstuff.

Natural habitat and behavior: Widely distributed, occurring in the upper levels of water, in rivers and streams. These cichlids live at higher densities than other larger species from this region, but still prove aggressive and territorial by nature. Pairs usually spawn under rocks, but will sometimes breed in a more exposed position. Typically, females lay about 100 eggs, which hatch within four days. The adult then takes the fry to a nearby pit in the substrate, guarding them ferociously. In some areas, it is not uncommon for groups of adult convict cichlids to cooperate to drive away would-be predators.

Aquarium conditions: Water at 68–73°F (20–23°C), with water chemistry being soft and slightly acid. Plants are likely to be dug up if not in pots. Rockwork and a clean clay pot are essential for spawning. Pairs differ in their choice of breeding sites, and also in terms of the degree of parental interest that they display. Even if they do not express interest in looking after a brood, the young cichlids will be able to survive on their own. This variation in behavior may be a reflection that strains have been bred in aquariums for almost 70 years.

AGASSIZ'S DWARF CICHLID

Apistogramma agassizii

Distribution: Occurs from Peru and Colombia almost to the vicinity of Belem, in tributaries of the Amazon, South America

Size: Up to 4in (10cm)

Form: Variable in color, even among wild populations. Those with prominent red coloration, especially on the caudal fin, occur in westerly areas, while yellow forms originate from more central as well as eastern areas of their distribution. The attractive blue-white variety is best known in waters around the Brazilian city of Manaus. Males are decidedly larger, more colorful and have more prominent, elongated fins. The caudal fin of females is of a much more rounded shape.

Diet: Omnivorous; will take flake food and other prepared foods but also needs live food.

Natural habitat and behavior: Occurring in rivers across a wide area, these fish are found in heavily vegetated stretches of water. A single male may maintain a territory containing several females, which is defended from other males. They spawn in caves, with females laying up to 150 eggs. These should hatch after four days, with the young cichlids starting to become free-swimming in a further four days or so.

Aquarium conditions: Water at 72–77°F (22–25°C), with the conditions being soft and acidic, about pH 6. Living naturally in river systems, these cichlids are not tolerant of any build-up of nitrogenous waste in their aquarium. Regular water changes are very important. The water must also be well oxygenated, like the river flow in their natural habitat. Overall, the tank must be well planted, with a dark substrate. If a male is kept in the company of two or more females, ensure the tank is large enough to incorporate retreats for each; otherwise, displays of aggression are inevitable. Clay pots are recommended for spawning sites.

⭐ BLUE ACARA (BLUE-SPOT CICHLID)

Aequidens pulcher

Distribution: Panama in Central America south to Colombia and northern Venezuela; also occurs on Trinidad.

Size: Up to 8in (20cm)

Form: There are

differences between the various populations, to the extent that some taxonomists group all of them together, while others recognize the Colombian forms as distinct species, described as *A. latifrons* or *A. caeruleopunctatus*. The underlying body color of these fish is yellowish-brown, with up to eight dark bands encircling the body. Bluish spots as well as streaks are apparent, with a variable yellow-red edge to the dorsal fin. Males

have a greater number of longer rays present at the back of their dorsal and anal fins, but this feature will not necessarily be apparent unless they are in top condition.

Diet: Carnivorous; diet should include live food.

Natural habitat and behavior: Territorial by nature, although not generally very aggressive, certainly in the case of captive-bred stock. They will dig in the substrate and may uproot plants here as a consequence, although they will not damage vegetation directly. Pairs form a strong pair bond, and clean the spawning site before the female lays up to 500 eggs. Both fish then guard the eggs, and watch over the fry when they hatch about three days later. They will be free-swimming in a further week or so.

Aquarium conditions: Water at 64–77°F (18–25°C) will be suitable, being raised slightly to encourage spawning. These cichlids are quite adaptable as to water chemistry, but regular water changes are important, especially in view of their diet. Aquarium plants should be kept in pots, and need to be relatively robust. Floating plants can also be useful, providing cover. Pairs will often spawn repeatedly, and the young cichlids are easy to rear, providing that the water quality in their aquarium is maintained. Sexual maturity is reached once they are about 2.5in (7cm) in length.

⭐ NICARAGUAN CICHLID (SPILOTUM)

Copora (Cichlasoma) nicaraguense

Distribution: Nicaragua, occurring in lakes Managua and Nicaragua, as well as the Rio San Juan, Costa Rica, Central America

Size: Up to 10in (25cm)

Form: Broad, curved head, with attractive pastel coloring. Typical light bluish, with darker pale violet line running down each side of the body. Underparts pale yellowish. Females in this case are more brightly colored, with a metallic gold upright dorsal fin. Males grow significantly larger and often develop signs of a hump on the head when they mature.

Diet: Omnivorous, eating a suitable commercial cichlid diet and live foods.

Natural habitat and behavior: Inhabit rocky areas, where there are plenty of suitable spawning retreats. What sets it apart from other *Cichlasoma* in which it was previously classified is that females produce around 500 non-adhesive eggs that are laid in a pit. This is typically concealed at the back of a retreat,

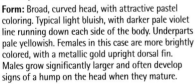

where they are closely guarded by the female alone. Males range farther afield, protecting the territory. Hatching takes place after about three days, and the young are free-swimming by five days old. Snails normally feature prominently in the diet of these cichlids in the wild.

Aquarium conditions: A pair will require a large aquarium, at least 4ft (1.2m) in length. Water at 73–82°F (23–28°C) is suitable; they are also reasonably adaptable in terms of water chemistry. A pH reading of 7–8 will be satisfactory; more importantly, the quality of the water needs to be good. Dark retreats are required to serve as spawning sites. Some pairs are more destructive toward vegetation than others, sometimes nibbling shoots, so only relatively robust plants should be chosen.

OLD WORLD AFRICAN AND ASIATIC SPECIES

Julidochromis ornatus

Distribution: The shoreline area of Lake Tanganyika, East Africa

Size: 3in (7.5cm)

Form: Slender-bodied, with three prominent dark brownish-black

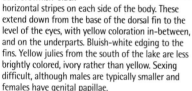

horizontal stripes on each side of the body. These extend down from the base of the dorsal fin to the level of the eyes, with yellow coloration in-between, and on the underparts. Bluish-white edging to the fins. Yellow julies from the south of the lake are less brightly colored, ivory rather than yellow. Sexing difficult, although males are typically smaller and females have genital papillae.

Diet: Mainly carnivorous, eating flake and other prepared foods, as well as suitable live food.

Natural habitat and behavior: Inhabit rocky areas, the small caves acting as retreats for these small but quite aggressive cichlids. They are not social by

nature, except for breeding pairs that can form a strong bond. Females spawn in a secure rocky retreat, producing few eggs—typically between 20 and 50, and never more than 100 with hatching occurring in three days. Pairs do not guard them closely, but their strong territorial instincts help to protect the eggs and fry. At first, the fry remain on the roof of the cave. They are free-swimming in a further five days.

Aquarium conditions: Medium-hard to hard water conditions, with a pH of 8–9. Water at 72–75°F (22–24°C). Rockwork required as a retreat and for spawning. Their small size means that a pair do not require a large setup, with a tank 18in (45cm) long adequate. Include tough plants such as Vallisnerias.

Neolamprologus (Lamprologus) brevis

Distribution: Occurs widely in Lake Tanganyika, East Africa

Size: Up to 2in (5cm)

Form: Fawn-brown coloration with variable

horizontal white barring on the flanks, with these bands being broader in some individuals than others. Degree of iridescence also apparent, notably below the eyes where there is a pale violet streak. There are also darker markings surrounding the eyes. Males are larger and more colorful, with a distinctive orange edging on the dorsal and caudal fins.

Diet: Small live foods and flake.

Natural habitat and behavior: These tiny cichlids range to considerable depths in the lake, down to 180ft (55m), in sandy areas where *Neothauma* snails are common. They occupy the shells of dead snails, which provide them with both retreats and spawning sites. The cichlids rearrange the position of the shell in the sandy substrate so they can gain access to it very rapidly if danger threatens. When spawning,

females partly retreat into their shells, the male then fertilizing the eggs within. Typically only 15–30 are laid, hatching out in a day, the young able to swim within a further week. They are watched over by the females until they are about two weeks old.

Aquarium conditions: Introduced to the aquarium hobby in 1979. These fish have proved reasonably adaptable in their choice of snail shells; those of edible snails (*Helix* species) sold in delicatessens are suitable. A sandy substrate, at least 2in (5cm) deep is essential so the shells can be partially buried. Water conditions should match those provided for julies (*Julidochromis ornatus*). They can usually be housed together as tankmates without problems. Brevis do establish a territory around their chosen shells, but this is no more than 8in (20cm) in diameter.

★ WHITE-SPOTTED CICHLID (DUBOISI)

Tropheus duboisi (M)

Distribution: Relatively shallow areas in northern Lake Tanganyika, East Africa

Size: 4.5in (12cm)

Form: The two races of this cichlid differ significantly in appearance. The broad yellow-banded form has been identified from the Malagarazi estuary, while the white-banded occurs north of Malagarazi and the Ubwari peninsula. They are otherwise dark in color, with characteristic banding extending down each side of the body to a variable extent, some distance behind the pectoral fins. Males are slightly larger, with longer pelvic fins. Young fish of this species are more colorful, having spots that match their banding.

Diet: Eat small live foods and plant matter; Also recommended are cichlid foods with a vegetarian bias plus fresh greenfood.

Natural habitat and behavior: Inhabit rocky areas, typically at depths of 8–41ft (3–15m). Females usually lay their eggs in spaces in the rocks before collecting them up again in their mouths. Although generally peaceful toward other species, these cichlids can be aggressive and territorial toward their own kind, proving to be relatively solitary by nature.

Aquarium conditions: Typical conditions match those required by other cichlids from this group of lakes, with the water needing to be both medium-hard and alkaline. The temperature range is 73–81°F (23–27°C). Rocks should feature prominently in the tank decor, and the aquarium itself can be well lit. This should serve to promote algal growth, which will allow the fish to browse on this plant matter, just as they do in their native habitat. Successful breeding in aquarium surroundings is not uncommon, although the number of eggs laid is small— typically between five and 15 at a single spawning. Once the young have hatched, they will continue darting back into their mother's mouth for a week or so, at the hint of any danger.

★ KRIBENSIS (PURPLE CICHLID)

Pelvicachromis pulcher

Distribution: Southern Nigeria, West Africa

Size: up to 4in (10cm)

Form: Females in this case are more brightly colored, with rounded anal fins and a yellow stripe in their dorsal fins. Males in contrast are larger overall, with their anal fins being pointed. There is a wide variation in coloration, between different forms. There are red, green, yellow, and blue morphs, with these colors being apparent to a greater or lesser extent on the lower half of the body. Colors generally brighten as the time for spawning approaches.

Diet: Eat a varied diet including flake, but also need live food; mosquito larvae favored.

Natural habitat and behavior: Frequently found in slightly brackish water. Occur in slow-flowing areas and connected ponds, where color morphs have developed, as relatively isolated populations. Territorial but not especially aggressive. Will excavate the substrate on occasions. Spawn on the roof of a suitable cave, where about 200 eggs may be laid over the course of an hour or so. Females carry freshly hatched fry to a spawning pit to watch over them for another week, as they grow and become free-swimming.

Aquarium conditions: A relatively large aquarium should be provided. Water conditions which are slightly on the acid side of neutral, and medium-hard are required by these cichlids, with a temperature in the range of 75–79°F (24–26°C). They need to be housed in a densely planted tank, incorporating cavelike retreats but with an open space for swimming as well. The substrate must not be too coarse; otherwise, the adult female will be unable to excavate a suitable pit for their fry in due course. Some breeders have used cleaned coconut halves, stripping off the outer husk and drilling holes in the sides, to act as cavelike spawning sites for these particular cichlids.

✪ JEWEL CICHLID

Hemichromis bimaculatus

Distribution: Southern Guinea to central Liberia, West Africa

Size: Up to 6in (15cm)

Form: Predominantly reddish, with dark, roughly circular markings edged with yellow on each side of the head just above and in front of the pectoral fin. There is also a blackish area midway along the body,

and a second blotched spot on the caudal peduncle. The remainder of the body coloration is reddish, more of a beige-brown shade on the upperparts and becoming more fiery overall when the fish are in spawning condition. Males have a number of golden-yellow spots on the sides of their heads.

Diet: Omnivorous, eating both prepared foods and live foods.

Natural habitat and behavior: Found in narrow watercourses where the water is clear, including forest streams. Become aggressive and highly territorial when spawning. The female typically produces 200–500 eggs at this stage, with the young usually hatching within two days and then being moved to pits where their parents continue to guard them. Several pits may be used in succession.

Aquarium conditions: Water needs to be soft and acidic to match that of their natural habitat, with frequent partial water changes being required to maintain its quality. The temperature should be within the range of 70–77°F (21–25°C). Rockwork is important, and should be surrounded by plants at the back of the tank. This should encourage these cichlids to spawn here in due course, often seeking out a flat rock which they clean beforehand for this purpose. Infusoria are helpful for rearing the fry. The young cichlids will be mature by the time they are 3in (7.5cm) long. Compatibility can be a problem in this species, but breeding usually occurs without problems once a pair bond is established, except that pairs may dig around in the substrate at this stage.

✪ LEMON CICHLID

Neolamprologus (Lamprologus) leleupi

Distribution: Around the northwest, west and eastern shores of Lake Tanganyika

Size: Up to 4.25in (11cm)

Form: Best known for their spectacular yellow coloration, with a relatively elongated, slim body. Sexing is difficult, but males may grow slightly larger, with a longer pelvic fin. The head may be thicker, with that of the female being less rounded and lacking any trace of a cranial hump. Three subspecies have been identified, from different parts of the lake. *N. l. longior* can be distinguished from the nominate subspecies *N. l. leleupi* by its slightly

longer body length, and more intense orange tone to its yellow body. *N. l. melas* from the northwest has a chestnut-brown body.

Diet: Carnivorous, eating live foods.

Natural habitat and behavior: Occur in rocky areas of coastline, preferring deeper waters around 110ft (40m). Captive-bred strains have lost some of their stunning coloration, which suggests that their diet may play a significant part in maintaining their appearance. They feed mainly in the wild on small shrimps taken off rocks, and possibly aquatic snails as well, crushing their shells with broad-surface molar teeth present on their pharyngeal bones. Females lay anywhere from about 50 to 150 eggs, on the roof of a cave. There is a strong pair bond, with the male staying outside and defending the territory, while the female watches over the eggs and fry.

Aquarium conditions: Water temperature 73–79°F (23–26°C), with the water medium hard and alkaline: pH 7.5–8.0. The tank should have a sandy bottom, with rockwork cave areas, suitable as retreats and for spawning purposes. Keep pairs together, and separate the young cichlids from their parents by six weeks old. Otherwise, they could be eaten.

⭐ MALAWI GOLDEN CICHLID

Melanochromis auratus

Distribution: Rocky areas in the southern part of Lake Malawi, East Africa. On the western shore, it extends to north Jalo Reef, but absent from the eastern side.

Form: Females are more colorful than males, being rather reminiscent of julie (*Julidochromis ornatus*) from Lake Tanganyika. They too have three dark horizontal stripes running down the side of their bodies, with the remainder of the body being silvery-yellow. Males in contrast are much darker, with the sides of their bodies being dark, split by a white stripe running down the center of the flanks.

They have yellow egg spots apparent on the anal fin. There are differences in depth of the coloration between different populations in the lake, with the most brightly colored examples being present around the lake islands of Maleri, Mbenji, and Mumbo.

Diet: Herbivorous diet, using a suitable cichlid food incorporating spirulina.

Natural habitat and behavior: Shallow rocky areas and in deeper water below 27ft (9m). They feed mainly on algae, nibbling this off rocks. Female fish are sometimes encountered in groups; males are territorial when in breeding condition. These are mouthbrooding cichlids, with females laying 20–30 eggs; These are fertilized and retained in the female's mouth until they hatch. The young will then dart back there for a week or so after becoming free-swimming.

Aquarium conditions: Medium-hard water, neutral to slightly alkaline pH and a water temperature of 72–79°F (22–26°C) being recommended. Add plenty of rockwork, which will not affect the water chemistry, as these cichlids are members of the so-called mbuna group. House several females with a single male in a species' tank, because of their polygamous nature.

⭐ TROPHEOPS

Pseudotropheus (Tropheops) tropheops

Distribution: Southern part of Lake Malawi, East Africa, extending from Chemwezi Rocks to Maleri Islands

Size: Up to 5in (14cm)

Form: The taxonomy of these mbuna cichlids is unresolved. A number of different variants at different localities around the lake are labeled under this general species name. Females vary from shades of yellow to beige, while darker males may display shades of brown to dark gray, often overlaid with a bluish suffusion, and combined with yellow egg spots on the anal fin.

Diet: Herbivorous, requiring a vegetarian-based cichlid diet.

Natural habitat and behavior: These fish use their strong mouthparts to feed on algae that they pull off rocks. Males maintain quite large breeding territories, with diameters ranging from 5 to 8ft (2–3 m). There are apparent variations in the level of aggression between the different forms of this species; one ('Tropheops Aggressive') recorded from a bay lying between Maytambukira and Chitands island, is considered to be particularly territorial, with both sexes driving away would-be intruders from their domains. Tropheops are mouthbrooders, typically laying up to 30 eggs. The female retains these in her mouth, with the young fry first emerging about three weeks later.

Aquarium conditions: Temperature between 73 and 79°F (23–26°C). The water chemistry is similar to that required by other Rift Valley cichlids, reflecting the geology of the region. Medium-hard to hard, with the pH in the alkaline part of the scale. Rockwork is again essential, with plants being of less significance and not always easy to cultivate successfully under these water conditions. Males should be housed apart, in the company of several females.

Pseudotropheus zebra

Distribution: East Africa, along the shoreline of northwest and western parts of Lake Malawi and a more limited distribution on the eastern side from Masinje south to Makanjila Point

Size: Up to in (13.5cm), with the biggest examples recorded from Makulawe Point, Likoma Island

Form: Populations vary, but typically bluish overall, more greenish on the lower side of the body, especially in the vicinity of the underside of the body. Yellow egg spots on the anal fin, and a burned gold color on the dorsal and top part of the caudal fin. One of the most colorful of the variants is *P.* sp. Zebra Gold; females in this case are orange-yellow, with males being browner in color. The tangerine Zebra is pictured. (See also page 79.)

Diet: Vegetarian cichlid food containing spirulina.

Natural habitat and behavior: Only occur in typically rocky areas, not where there is a combination of rocks and sand. Typically position themselves at 45 degrees to the horizontal when feeding on algae growing on rocks, levering this off with its strong jaws. May also consume plankton when swimming in open water. Those occurring in areas where there is a lot of sediment are less heavily barred than those living where the waters are clearer, suggesting that this feature gives them camouflage.

Aquarium conditions: Again, medium-hard, alkaline water heated to 73–79°F (23–26°C). Breeding groups should comprise a male and several females, although it is usually possible to keep odd individuals in the company of other nonaggressive species from the lake. Females lay relatively large clutches of up to 60 eggs. The young first leave the safety of their mother's mouth at three weeks old.

Aulonocara "nyassae"

Distribution: East Africa. Present in the vicinity of Fort Maguire and north of Masinje in Lake Malawi, as well as probably Mara Point and on the Mozambique shoreline as well.

Size: Up to 4in (10cm)

Form: There is confusion over the exact identity of the fish described under this name, as scientifically, it is known as *A. hansbaenschi*. First discovered in 1987 from the vicinity of Fort Maguire, it is predominantly blue, often with darker markings on the body and sometimes with reddish coloration in the vicinity of the pectoral fins. Males of the same population tend to be more brightly colored than females.

Diet: Carnivorous, with live food needed.

Natural habitat and behavior: Typically occur at depths of 19ft (6m) and tend to be quite shy, living in caves. Males are strongly territorial, and excavate caves beneath rocks. Females are relatively social often associating in groups, as do young males before they establish territories. They feed on a variety of invertebrates collected in the sand.

Aquarium conditions: Alkaline and medium-hard water conditions are again vital for these fish, with a temperature of 72–77°F (22–25°C) being maintained. The digging behavior of males means that plants are likely to be uprooted, and so these should be set in pots. Only relatively robust plants are likely to thrive in this type of water, so that overall, plastic plants can be useful for this type of environment. The substrate must not be too coarse, preventing the male fish from excavating the caves, which serve to attract females in spawning condition. The female starts to collect up her eggs as they are laid, and picks at the egg spots on the anal fin, which encourages the male to release his sperm, fertilizing the eggs in her mouth. Her mouth provides a sanctuary for the young after hatching.

⭐ BLUE DOLPHIN

Cyrtocara (*Haplochromis*) *moorii*

Distribution: Most common in southern areas of Lake Malawi, but occur all around this East African lake; also present in nearby Lake Malombe.

Size: 9in (23cm)

Form: Unusually in this case, particularly given the wide range of this species, no local variants are recognized. Predominantly blue in color. It is not possible to sex these fish visually with complete certainty, although generally, mature males have larger humps on their foreheads than females.

Diet: Omnivorous, but prefer live foods.

Natural habitat and behavior: Occur in sandy rather than rocky areas of the lake, typically at depths of 8–41ft (3–15m), and are largely dependent on the efforts of other fish to obtain food. Blue dolphins follow the larger insectivorous *Lethrinops* (*Taeniolethrinops*) *praeorbitalis* over the substrate, seeking to feed on particles which its bigger companion has excavated with its long snout. Shadowing sessions of this type may last for over half an hour, typically involving just one fish of each species. Sometimes, however, young blue dolphins may accompany an older individual. Adults are aggressive toward another species, *Protomelas annectens*, which has a similar lifestyle but is slightly smaller.

Aquarium conditions: Ideally should include one of their feeding companions, and a sandy base, to encourage them to display their natural feeding behavior, but this is often not possible, and demands a large tank. In other respects, the type of setup required by blue dolphins does not differ significantly from that needed by other Lake Malawian cichlids. A male should be housed in the company of several females, who may each produce 20–90 eggs, fertilized on the substrate and brooded in their mouths. Good water quality is vital to the fry's health.

⭐ ORANGE CHROMIDE

Etroplus maculatus

Distribution: Western India and Sri Lanka

Size: 3in (7.5cm)

Form: Yellowish background color, with darker black markings on the lower part of

the body, and a similar prominent spot about halfway down each flank. Small orange dots extend in lines down the sides of these cichlids. Sexing is quite difficult, but females tend not to be so brightly colored, and show no trace of a reddish edge to their fins. There is a bluish variant, where light blue coloration replaces the black; and some are distinctly more brightly colored than the norm.

Diet: Live foods preferred but will take a suitable cichlid diet and freeze-dried invertebrates.

Natural habitat and behavior: Cichlids are not widespread in Asia, and this species is quite unusual in that it is frequently encountered in brackish water. A female lays between 200 and 300 eggs, often on rocks. The young cichlids are then transferred to pits by the adults, and guarded, with both fish being actively involved in caring for their offspring. It has been suggested that they may produce a body mucus that the fry nibble at, once they are free-swimming.

Aquarium conditions: A well-planted tank, which also incorporates open areas for swimming. Flat rocks, which will not affect the water chemistry, are recommended as possible spawning sites. The water temperature range is 68–79°F (20–26°C), being increased slightly to encourage spawning. It should be medium-hard, with the pH being in the range of neutral to slightly alkaline. It will help, especially if a pair does spawn, to have added marine salt at the rate of one teaspoonful per gallon (3.8l) to the aquarium water at the outset, as well as when carrying out partial water changes. This lessens the likelihood of the fry in particular succumbing to fungal infections.

Further Reading

Alderton, David, *The International Encyclopedia of Tropical Freshwater Fish* (Howell Book House, New York, USA, 1997).

Andrews, Chris, Excell, A., and Carrington, N., *The Manual of Fish Health* (Salamander Books, London, UK, 1988).

Axelrod, Herbert R., and Burgess, Warren E., *African Cichlids of Lakes Malawi and Tanganyika* (TFH Publications, Neptune, USA, 1988).

Barlow, George W., *The Cichlid Fishes: Nature's Grand Experiment in Evolution* (Perseus Publishing, Cambridge, USA, 2000).

Britchard, Pierre, *Cichlids and all the Other Fishes of Lake Tanganyika* (TFH Publications, Neptune, USA, 1989).

Dawes, John, *Complete Encyclopedia of the Freshwater Aquarium* (Firefly, Ontario, Canada, 2001).

Glaser, U., and Glaser, W., *South American Cichlids: Vols 1–3* (Verlag A.C.S., GmbH, Morfelden-Walldorf, Germany, 1996).

Gobel, M., and Mayland, H.J., *South American Cichlids IV—Discus, Scalare* (Verlag A.C.S., GmbH, Morfelden-Walldorf, Germany, 1998).

Goldschmidt, Tijs, *Darwin's Dreampond: Drama in Lake Victoria* (MIT Press, Cambridge, USA, 1998).

Kingdon, John, *Island Africa* (Collins, London, UK, 1990).

Konings, Ad, *Cichlids from Central America* (TFH Publications, Neptune, USA, 1989).

Konings, Ad, *Cichlids and all the Other Fishes of Lake Malawi* (TFH Publications, Neptune, USA, 1990).

Linke, H., and Staeck, W., *Cichlids from West Africa* (Tetra, Blacksburg, USA, 1994).

Mayland, H.J., and Bork, D., *South American Dwarf Cichlids:* Apistogramma, Crenicara, Microgeophagus (Verlag A.C.S., GmbH, Morfelden-Walldorf, Germany, 1998).

Richter, Hans-Joachim, *Complete Book of Dwarf Cichlids* (TFH, Neptune, USA, 1989).

Smith, Mark Philip, *Lake Tanganyikan Cichlids* (Barron's, New York, USA, 1998).

Smith, Mark Philip, *Lake Victoria Basin Cichlids* (Barron's, New York, USA, 2001).

Staeck, W., and Linke, H., *Cichlids from Eastern Africa* (Tetra, Blacksburg, USA, 1994).

Zurlo, Georg, *The Tanganyika Cichlid Aquarium* (Barron's, New York, USA, 2000).

Websites:

Cichlids of Central America
http://www.cichlid.nl/
South & Central American cichlids: House of Cichlids
http://www.viaje.net.ph/benedick/
All cichlids, especially African: Cybercichlids
http://www.cybercichlids.com
Tanganyikan Cichlids
http://www.tanganyikan-cichlids.co.uk/

Glossary

Acidic A reading on the **pH** scale below 7.0.

Adaptive radiation The way in which species change their lifestyles to avoid competition and occupy their own niche.

Adsorb The way in which molecules may adhere to a porous surface such as carbon, which can help to filter out some unwanted substances in aquarium water.

Algae Microscopic plants present in water, which can coat glass, rockwork and other surfaces in the aquarium, especially under strong light.

Alkaline A reading on the **pH** scale measuring above 7.0.

Anal fin Unpaired fin in front of the vent.

Aufwuchs Mats of **algae**, which provide food for some cichlids.

Biotope The fish's immediate natural environment.

Blackwater extract Commercially available preparations that mimic the soft, acidic water conditions prevalent in the Amazonian region.

Brackish Water conditions that are more saline than freshwater, but are not as salty as seawater itself. Typically encountered at the mouths of estuaries.

Cable tidy, or power strip A connecting block that can take a number of electrical outputs from the aquarium and joins to the main supply through a single plug.

Calciferous Rock containing calcium carbonate.

Caudal fin The tail fin.

Cephalic hump See **nuchal hump.**

Chemical filtration Typically describes the use of activated carbon to remove harmful substances.

Chromosomes The strands on which the genes are located in the nucleus of cells.

Cone cells Cells present on the retina at the back of the eye that facilitate color vision.

Crown The center of a plant, from where new growth occurs.

Dechlorinator A product that removes harmful chlorine from local water supplies, making it safe for the fish; may not always be effective against chloramine.

Delayed mouthbrooders Cichlids such as *Satanoperca* spp. that do not collect their eggs immediately after spawning, collecting them up instead after a day or so. *See also* **mouthbrooder.**

Dorsal fin The prominent fin which lies farthest forward on the upper area of the back.

Dropsy Abnormal swelling of the body. May have infectious or non-infectious causes.

Egg spots Ovoid markings on the anal fins of some male cichlids that resemble eggs in appearance and are significant in the breeding process, attracting the female here so fertilization can occur.

Family A group of fish that consists of members of different genera.

Filter bed The medium, such as gravel, through which water passes as part of the filtration process.

Flake Prepared food for fish that floats well on the water surface, being very thin.

Free-swimming The stage at which young fish start to swim around their quarters for the first time.

Genital papillae Small projections around the genital opening of some cichlids.

Genus Group of closely related fish consisting of one or more species.

GH Reflects the general or permanent hardness of a water sample. Unaffected by boiling the water.

Gills The means by which fish are able to extract oxygen from the water (though not the only means). Membranes well supplied with blood vessels located just behind the eyes on each side of the head.

Hard water Water that contains a relatively high level of dissolved calcium or magnesium salts.

Heaterstat Combined heater and thermostat unit for aquarium use.

Hemoglobin Oxygen-carrying pigment located in the red blood cells.

Herptile Relating to reptiles and amphibians.

Hormone Chemical messenger produced in the body and carried through the blood to act on other organs.

Hybridization Mating between different species, giving rise to hybrid offspring that display characteristics of both parents.

KH A measure of temporary hardness, resulting from bicarbonates or carbonates dissolved in the water, which can be reduced by boiling.

Ichthyologists Those who study fish.

Labial Refers to the lips.

Lateral line A sensory system running down the sides of the fish's body, allowing it to sense vibrations in the water.

Lekking A group of male fish displaying at a particular site in the hope of attracting a female partner.

Length Measurements of fish are usually carried out in a straight line from the snout to the base of the caudal fin, which is itself excluded.

Lepidophage A fish that eats the scales of other fish.

Mbuna The local Chichewa tribal description for rock-dwelling cichlids found in Lake Malawi.

Mechanical filtration The direct removal of waste matter by filtration, which sieves it out of the water.

Microhabitats Small, localized areas of habitats differing from adjacent areas.

Monogamous A one-to-one pairing system of a male and female. *See also* **Polygamous**.

Mouthbrooder A fish that retains its fertilized eggs in its mouth until they hatch, and may also allow its young back there for a period afterwards to escape danger.

Mulm The debris that can accumulate on the floor of the aquarium.

Mutation A genetically induced change in color or appearance.

Nauplii The larval stage in the life-cycle of the brine shrimp *Artemia*, cultured as a rearing food for young fish.

New Tank Syndrome Describes the potential for sudden death of aquarium occupants resulting from a fatal build-up of ammonia and nitrite in a newly-established tank where the filtration system is not working effectively.

Nitrogen cycle The breakdown of toxic ammonia produced by the fish through nitrite and less toxic nitrate, which is used by plants for healthy growth.

Nocturnal Describes fish that are active after dark.

Nuchal hump Swelling on the head, most commonly seen in some mature male cichlids. Also known as the **cephalic hump**.

Operculum The movable flap that covers the **gills**, and allows water to flow over them.

Pectoral fin Paired fins located on each side of the body behind the gills.

Pelvic fin Fin present in front of the anal fin.

pH The relative acidity or alkalinity of a solution, based on a logarithmic scale, so each unit change represents a tenfold alteration in concentration, with pH 7 being neutral. Low values reflect increasing acidity; higher figures indicate a progressively more alkaline solution.

Pharyngeal teeth Sharp projections used for rasping food, located in the pharynx region of some fish at the back of the mouth.

Photosynthesis Process by which plants manufacture their nutritional requirements using light.

Piscivorous Describes fish that hunt other fish for food.

Pit Area in the **substrate** where spawning takes place and some young cichlids are corralled by their parents.

Polygamous Describes a male that mates with several females, rather than as a member of a pair. See also **Monogamous**.

Polymorphism Occurrence of the same species in recognizably distinctive forms.

Power filter A filtration unit that incorporates its own pump to drive water through the unit.

Quarantine The complete isolation of newly-acquired fish for a period of time, to ensure they are healthy, before introducing them to others.

Rays Parts of the bony framework that provide the structural support for the fins.

Reverse osmosis A process that alters water chemistry by removing dissolved salts, resulting in pure water. Often abbreviated to R.O.

Schools Cichlid groups, usually of one species, swimming together.

Semi-circular canals Organ of balance in the inner ear.

Soft water Water low in dissolved salts; includes most rainwater.

Spawning The process of mating and egg-laying.

Species A group of fish that closely resemble each other and can interbreed to produce fertile offspring. Alternative definitions are defended by some biologists.

Spirulina A type of algae, often utilized as fish food.

Substrate The floor covering in the aquarium or the base of the fish's natural habitat.

Swim bladder The fish's air-filled organ of buoyancy.

Taxonomy The science of identifying fish and unravelling their relationships.

Territorial Describes cichlids that establish and defend a territory.

Tomite The free-swimming, infective stage of the microscopic parasite that causes white spot.

Trace element Inorganic chemicals that are needed in small amounts for healthy plant and fish growth. Present in the water or in food.

Undergravel filter A plate filter that fits right across the bottom of the aquarium.

Vent Ano-genital opening behind the anal fin.

Yolk sac Source of nourishment for fry prior to and immediately after hatching.

Index